The Crusades
Failed Holy Wars

Titles in the History's Great Defeats series include:

The Aztecs: End of a Civilization
The British Empire: The End of Colonialism
The Cold War: Collapse of Communism
The Indian Wars: From Frontier to Reservation
The Third Reich: Demise of the Nazi Dream

The Crusades
Failed Holy Wars

by Cherese Cartlidge

Lucent Books, San Diego, CA

Library of Congress Cataloging-in-Publication Data

Cartlidge, Cherese.
  The Crusades : failed holy wars / by Cherese Cartlidge.
    p. cm. — (History's great defeats)
  Includes bibliographical references and index.
  ISBN 1-56006-999-6 (hardback : alk. paper)
  1. Crusades. 2. Aggressiveness—Religious aspects. 3. Religious tolerance—History—To 1500. 4. Middle East—History. 5. Europe—Church history—600–1500. 6. Jews—Persecutions—Europe, Western. 7. Christianity and other religions. 8. Religion and civilization. I. Title. II. Series.
  D160 .C37   2002
  909'07—dc21

2001004293

Table of Contents

Foreword

HISTORY IS FILLED with tales of dramatic encounters that sealed the fates of empires or civilizations, changing them or causing them to disappear forever. One of the best known events began in 334 B.C., when Alexander, king of Macedonia, led his small but formidable Greek army into Asia. In the short span of only ten years, he brought Persia, the largest empire the world had yet seen, to its knees, earning him the nickname forever after associated with his name—"the Great." The demise of Persia, which at its height stretched from the shores of the Mediterranean Sea in the west to the borders of India in the east, was one of history's most stunning defeats. It occurred primarily because of some fatal flaws in the Persian military system, disadvantages the Greeks had exploited before, though never as spectacularly as they did under Alexander.

First, though the Persians had managed to conquer many peoples and bring huge territories under their control, they had failed to create an individual fighting man who could compare with the Greek hoplite. A heavily armored infantry soldier, the hoplite fought in a highly effective and lethal battlefield formation—the phalanx. Possessed of better armor, weapons, and training than the Persians, Alexander's soldiers repeatedly crushed their Persian opponents. Second, the Persians for the most part lacked generals of the caliber of their Greek counterparts. And when Alexander invaded, Persia had the added and decisive disadvantage of facing one of the greatest generals of all time. When the Persians were defeated, their great empire was lost forever.

Other world powers and civilizations have fallen in a like manner. They have succumbed to some combination of inherent fatal flaws or disadvantages, to political and/or military mistakes, and even to the personal failings of their leaders.

Another of history's great defeats was the sad demise of the North American Indian tribes at the hands of encroaching European civilization from the sixteenth to nineteenth centuries. In this case, all of the tribes suffered from the same crippling disadvantages. Among the worst, they lacked the great numbers, the unity, and the advanced industrial and military hardware possessed by the Europeans. Still another example, one closer to our own time, was the resounding defeat of Nazi Germany by the Allies in 1945, which brought World War II, the most disastrous conflict in history, to a close. Nazi Germany collapsed for many reasons. But one of the most telling was that its leader, Adolf Hitler, sorely underestimated the material resources and human resolve of the Allies, especially the United States. In the end, Germany was in a very real sense submerged by a massive and seemingly relentless tidal wave of Allied bombs, tanks, ships, and soldiers.

Seen in retrospect, a good many of the fatal flaws, drawbacks, and mistakes that caused these and other great defeats from the pages of history seem obvious. It is only natural to wonder why, in each case, the losers did not realize their limitations and/or errors sooner and attempt to avert disaster. But closer examination of the events, social and political trends, and leading personalities involved usually reveals that complex factors were at play. Arrogance, fear, ignorance, stubbornness, innocence, and other attitudes held by nations, peoples, and individuals often colored and shaped their reactions, goals, and strategies. And it is both fascinating and instructive to reconstruct how such attitudes, as well as the fatal flaws and mistakes themselves, contributed to the losers' ultimate demise.

Each volume in Lucent Books' *History's Great Defeats* series is designed to provide the reader with diverse learning tools for exploring the topic at hand. Each well-informed, clearly written text is supported and enlivened by substantial quotes by the actual people involved, as well as by later historians and other experts; and these primary and secondary sources are carefully documented. Each volume also supplies the reader with an extensive Works Consulted list, guiding him or her to further research on the topic. These and other research tools, including glossaries and time lines, afford the reader a thorough understanding of how and why one of history's most decisive defeats occurred and how these events shaped our world.

The Soldiers of Christ

Introduction

THE CRUSADERS CAME from England, Germany, Austria, Italy, and France. During the twelfth and thirteenth centuries, thousands upon thousands of these men, women, and children left behind their homes, families, and all that was familiar to them to join a great march eastward. The lucky ones had horses to carry them and their possessions, but most people had to walk, carrying sacks containing food, blankets, and other necessities over their shoulders. Some of them marched in their bare feet. These masses of people journeyed hundreds of miles over dangerous territory that included perilous mountains, swift rivers, and barren deserts. They cooked, ate, and slept outdoors in all kinds of weather. Many died from disease, accidents, and cold. Some of them attempted the journey by sea, only to perish in shipwrecks. Armed with clubs, axes, daggers, swords, and lances, these people were the warriors of the Crusades—wars that Christians waged in the name of God to gain control of the Holy Land from the Muslims who had controlled the area since the mid–seventh century.

The Crusades involved people of all classes in medieval Europe, from the lowliest serf to the landed noble all the way up to the pope—the head of the Church. For two centuries, every single generation in western Europe received a summons to go on crusade. Everyone in western Europe was touched by the Crusades in one way or another, whether by hearing a sermon on the Holy War, making a vow to go on crusade, contributing money or paying special taxes to finance the effort, or having a family member or neighbor who had made the long and dangerous trek to the Holy Land. Every city and village was drawn into the crusading movement, and by the close of the thirteenth century, there could not have been a soul alive in western Europe who had not been affected by the Crusades.

The sheer number of people who fought in the Crusades is staggering. A woman who lived in Constantinople (now called Istanbul, the capital of present-day Turkey) described the huge mass of people she saw as the first army of crusaders approached her city on its way to the Holy Land in 1096:

> Full of enthusiasm and ardour they thronged every highway, and with these warriors came a host of civilians, outnumbering the sand of the sea shore or the stars of heaven, carrying palms and bearing crosses on their shoulders. There were women and children, too, who had left their own countries. Like tributaries joining a river from all directions they streamed towards us in full force.[1]

Why did so many thousands of people stream out of Europe and risk being killed, wounded, or bankrupt to fight in a faraway land? While the motivations for joining the Crusades were diverse, most people who took the cross (made a vow to go on a crusade) were filled with a religious enthusiasm that in many cases verged on fanaticism. With red cloth crosses sewn to their clothing, and duty and faith foremost on their minds, the crusaders fought for a vast cause:

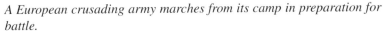

A European crusading army marches from its camp in preparation for battle.

to win control of the Holy Land—particularly Jerusalem—from the
Muslims. Europeans saw Muslims as the "enemies of Christ" and retaking the Holy Land—the place where Christ lived and died—as
their sacred duty. A French song from the Second Crusade echoes
this sense of duty in its opening lines:

> Chevalier, mult estes guariz,
> Quant Deu a vus fait sa clamur
> Des Turs e des Amoraviz,
> Ki li unt fait tels deshenors.[2]

These words implore Europe's knights to fight for the honor of
their God and promise eternal salvation to the brave knights who
defeat the enemy—the Muslim Turks. The enemy, the song continues, are accused of stealing Christianity's holiest sites.

During the First Crusade, the Christians managed to conquer much
of the Holy Land in swift order, occupying a narrow strip along the western coast of the Arabian Peninsula. They built castles and set up kingdoms there that were settled by crusaders and immigrants from Europe.
Although the Crusades were initially successful in achieving the primary
goal of conquering the Holy Land, in time they would suffer a prolonged
and disastrous defeat. Over the next two centuries, the Franks, as these
settlers were called, gradually lost all the castles they had built and all
the cities they had occupied as wave after wave of Muslim armies drove
them out of the Holy Land.

Despite the mammoth effort put into capturing the Holy Land,
the Crusades ended in catastrophic failure. They were a massive
movement, involving many peoples and countries and spanning a
great length of time. The Crusades were also a tragedy because they
cost so much money and took so many lives. One thirteenth-century
chronicler of the Crusades lamented the loss of life during this time:

> On this sort of pilgrimage against the Muslims countless
> people die, sometimes from sickness at sea, sometimes in
> battle, sometimes from a lack or excess of food; not only the
> common people, but also kings and princes and persons who
> do great service to Christianity. How much harm was done
> through the death of King Louis [IX of France], whose life
> was so beneficial to the Church of God, and through the
> deaths of many others![3]

Frankish soldiers leave the battlefield after being defeated by the Muslims.

Twenty years after the last crusade ended, the final crusader castles and cities fell to the Muslim armies, and the Christians left the Holy Land in defeat. Although there was talk in Europe over the next few centuries of sending further crusading expeditions to recover the Holy Land, Europeans would not set foot there in force again until the end of World War I—over six centuries later. While the crusaders failed to achieve their objective of permanently taking back the Holy Land, for two hundred years they had ruled the coastline of Asia Minor and been masters of the land they had set out to conquer, and for a brief time they had come very close to achieving their aim.

The Crusading Movement

Chapter 1

T HE CRUSADES WERE a series of military expeditions that European Christians waged during the Middle Ages against the perceived enemies of Christendom—the followers of Islam, called Muslims. Between 1096 and 1270, eight major crusades set out for the Holy Land under the direction of the pope, the head of the Western Church. The crusading movement came about because of a convergence of religious, political, social, and economic factors prevalent in western Europe during the Middle Ages. The same factors that helped bring about the Crusades also contributed to their failure.

Feudal Society

Western Europe at the time of the Crusades consisted of many individual kingdoms loosely under the central authority of a king. Each of these kingdoms was made up of smaller fiefdoms under the control of barons, dukes, and other nobles who were vassals, or tenants, of the king. These vassals pledged loyalty and military service to the king in exchange for a fief—a grant of land over which the noble ruled. In addition, a noble could have knights and other lesser nobles as vassals of his own, who had taken a similar oath of loyalty to him in exchange for a fief. These knights and lesser nobles then divided their property into smaller fiefs that they granted to their vassals, and so on down the line to village lords, whose fiefs consisted of a single village or manor. This system of dividing property into fiefs in exchange for loyalty and service was known as feudalism, and it created a hierarchy of power that extended from the lowliest peasant all the way up to the king.

The manor was the most basic feature of feudal society. The small villages were surrounded by farms, with the lord's castle or manor house at the center. Each manor within a kingdom retained a degree of autonomy, and the lord of each manor was the supreme authority for that manor. Each manor was protected by an army made up of knights and foot soldiers in the service of the lord. Thus, when a king wanted to go to war against a rival kingdom, he summoned all the nobles and knights in his service, who in turn issued the call to arms to all their vassals and their vassals' vassals. In this way enormous armies could be raised quickly.

With so many separate, and often rival, small kingdoms with their own authority, European society was very unstable. The feudal system was built around getting and keeping power by military means. It was quite common for rival kingdoms to attack one another as their rulers sought more lands for themselves, and day-to-day life in villages consisted of either defending against an attacker or attacking someone else. In addition, because of the practice of primogeniture, in which the eldest son of a king or noble inherited the title and land of his father, the younger sons of nobles were left landless and often resorted to attacking another kingdom (or even their own) in a grab for power and land. As historian Malcolm Billings explains,

A peasant is pictured here shearing a sheep for his lord.

"It was a time when political power was fragmented and armed bands roamed the countryside; petty nobles often became local tyrants, oppressing the peasants and savagely raiding each others' castles."[4] This situation meant that European kingdoms were in an almost constant state of war with one another during the Middle Ages.

The Life of a Peasant

Feudal society offered protection to impoverished peasants who would otherwise have no way to defend themselves against invasion from a rival kingdom or even a rival manor within their own kingdom. Despite this protection, life for most western Europeans during the Middle Ages was difficult and often unpleasant. The vast majority of the population consisted of peasants living on land owned by a feudal lord. From the time they were old enough to work in a field, these peasants had to work the land, toiling from dawn to dusk. Most years their farming produced barely enough to provide the basic necessities for themselves, and most of the meager money they earned was collected by the lord in taxes.

Peasants toil in this woodcut from 1517.

A peasant's life tended to be short—most died before the age of forty. Most families had lost one or more children to famine, accidents, or disease. Most peasants in Europe at that time were uneducated and illiterate, with little or no hope of escaping the dreary, grim realities of their daily lives. The land they worked belonged to the lord of the manor, and they had no way to obtain farms of their own. Peasants also had very little control over their own lives. The lord of the manor had the final say in all things, including what people's jobs would be, when they would work, and where they were allowed to travel—some peasants never left their own villages.

Religion played a large role in the daily life of medieval peasants; it offered them a means to cope with the hardships of their existence. The same could be said for the other members of medieval European society. Events beyond their control or understanding were explained as being acts of God. If they prospered because a harvest was good, people believed God was rewarding them for their righteousness. If they suffered because there was a drought, people believed God was punishing them for their sins. Peasants, knights, nobles, and kings devoted time each day to worship and other religious duties.

Pilgrimages and the Importance of the Holy Land

An important feature of medieval religion was pilgrimage. During the Middle Ages, Christians venerated the physical remains, or relics, of saints and martyrs. Shrines were built in Europe to house items such as the bones of an apostle or a lock of hair from a saint. People made pilgrimages, or journeys, to visit these shrines. The belief was that by undertaking a pilgrimage, people could gain absolution, or forgiveness, for their sins. Because sin was thought to be unavoidable, and medieval Christians feared that without absolution they were doomed to suffer unending torment in hell for their sins, many undertook arduous and lengthy pilgrimages to holy places as penance for their sins.

The most important relics and holy sites were those associated with Christ. These included the cup from which he drank at the Last Supper and a piece of wood from the cross on which he died. To walk in Christ's footsteps was considered one of the holiest actions a Christian could perform. Places in the Holy Land that were associated with Christ's birth, life, and death were therefore revered and became very popular destinations for Christian pilgrims. The ancient

The Relic Collection of King Louis IX

Relics, or objects that were associated with saints or martyrs, were highly venerated during the crusading era. The most sought-after relics in Europe were those associated with Christ himself. France's King Louis IX acquired the Crown of Thorns, assumed to be the one worn by Christ during the Crucifixion, for an enormous amount of money from the king of Jerusalem in 1239. To this relic he later added a piece of wood thought to be from the Holy Cross on which Christ was crucified. In Elizabeth Hallam's book *Four Gothic Kings*, Matthew Paris, a thirteenth-century English historian, describes Louis's collection of relics associated with Christ:

> The Holy Cross was brought to the kingdom of France through the careful arrangements, with Christ's help, of Louis IX, king of France, and his mother, Blanche of Castile. The enormous sum of twenty-five thousand pounds was paid by Louis to the Saracens of Damietta for the Holy Cross.
>
> The king of France ordered a chapel to be built in Paris near his palace, to be called the Sainte-Chapelle, marvelously beautiful and a fitting receptacle for this treasure, which he later deposited there with due honour. Besides this, the king kept in this magnificent chapel Christ's cloak, the spear (that is, the spearhead), the sponge and countless other relics.

Louis paid handsomely for these relics as well as for the building of the lavish Sainte-Chapelle. The cost of his relic collection and the huge amount of money he spent financing his crusades left debts that burdened the French government well past the king's death.

King Louis IX receives Christ's Crown of Thorns, one of the many relics in the king's collection.

city of Jerusalem was a holy city to Christians because it was where Christ had died. Jerusalem was home to the Church of the Holy Sepulchre, built on the site of Christ's tomb, and was a favorite destination for Christian pilgrims by the eleventh century. Many of these pilgrims passed through the territory of the vast Byzantine Empire on their way to the Holy Land.

The Byzantine Empire

During the Middle Ages, the most powerful Christian realm was the Byzantine Empire. Its territory spread across most of eastern Europe and much of Asia Minor, including modern-day Turkey, Greece, and northern Iran. Byzantium was the richest empire in the world, with an economy based on international trade rather than agriculture. The capital was Constantinople, which boasted paved streets, running water, and spectacular buildings and castles. The citizens of Constantinople and other Byzantine cities enjoyed a level of education and prosperity unknown in Europe at the time.

Just as there were Western and Eastern empires, based in Europe and Byzantium respectively, there were also two branches of Christianity. The Western Church was based in Rome and led by the pope, and the Eastern (or Orthodox) Church was based in Constantinople and led by the patriarch of Constantinople. There were many differences between the two branches of Christianity, including languages, customs, and theology. These differences led to a schism, or split, in 1054, in which Pope Leo IX excommunicated the head of the Orthodox Church, Patriarch Michael Cerularius. After the schism of 1054, the rift between the two branches of Christianity continued to widen.

The leaders of the Western and Eastern Churches each wanted their church to be the supreme authority over all of Christendom. The papacy wanted to reunite the two branches under the single authority of the Western Church, with the pope exerting control over all of Europe and Byzantium. At the same time, the pope also wanted to find a way to stop the epidemic of violence in western Europe and put the warring kings and knights under his power. It just so happened that events in Asia Minor in the latter part of the eleventh century presented Pope Urban II with the opportunity to spread his sphere of influence across Europe to Byzantium and beyond.

Pope Leo IX, head of the Church at the time of the schism of 1054.

An Appeal from the Byzantine Emperor

In the eleventh century a new power swept through Asia Minor—the Seljuq Turks. The Turks were a nomadic tribe from central Asia who had converted to Islam. In 1071 the Turks captured Jerusalem from the Arab Muslims who had ruled the city since 638. The Arabs had been tolerant of other religions and allowed Christian pilgrims access to the city's holy places. But the Turks, who soon gained control of most of Asia Minor, began to pose a threat to the safety of Christian pilgrims, robbing and even murdering them as they traveled through the Holy Land.

For centuries Byzantium had acted as protector for pilgrims and for Christian inhabitants of the Holy Land. But the Turks posed a serious threat to the stability of the Byzantine Empire. By the late eleventh century they had conquered most of the Byzantine provinces in Asia Minor and were getting dangerously close to the Byzantine capital. When the Turks conquered the Byzantine city of Nicaea in 1092 and turned it into their own capital, they were only fifty miles from Constantinople.

The presence of the Turks so close to Constantinople was cause for concern not only to Byzantium but also to Europe. If Byzantium fell to the Muslims it would give them a gateway into Europe. For centuries, the Byzantine Empire had helped to protect Europe from Muslim expansion. But now the Turkish army installed at Nicaea was less than three days' march from Constantinople.

Responding to the threats posed by the Turks, the Byzantine emperor Alexius I Comnenus sent envoys in March 1095 to appeal to Pope Urban II for assistance in holding off the Turks. After hearing Alexius's appeal, Urban devised a plan on a much grander scale than Alexius had imagined—a holy war, or crusade. Urban preached the idea in a sermon to an enormous crowd at the Council of Clermont in France the following November, saying:

> A grave report has come from the lands around Jerusalem and from the city of Constantinople. . . . A foreign race, a

Pope Urban II makes his great sermon at the Council of Clermont in support of the First Crusade.

Urban's Sermon at Clermont

In November 1095 at the Council of Clermont in France, Pope Urban II first preached the idea of a crusade to expel Muslims from the Holy Land. The crowd that gathered to hear the sermon was so large it would not fit inside the Clermont cathedral, and Urban had to preach in a field outside the eastern gate of the city. In his sermon Urban fused two very powerful motivators in the lives of medieval Europeans—pilgrimage to Jerusalem and holy war against the Muslims—thereby launching the First Crusade. The text of the sermon that changed the course of world history has not survived, but many eyewitness accounts were recorded later. The following account by Robert the Monk, written fifteen years after the sermon, is reprinted in Elizabeth Hallam's *Chronicles of the Crusades*.

> Jerusalem is the navel of the world, a land which is fruitful above all others, like another paradise of delights. The redeemer of the human race [Jesus] illuminated this land by his coming, graced it by his living there, made it holy by his suffering, redeemed it by his death, distinguished it by his burial. This royal city, set in the center of the world, is now held captive by its enemies and is enslaved in heathen rite by people who do not know God. Therefore the city demands and desires to be set free, and calls upon you without ceasing to come to its assistance. Indeed Jerusalem requires your support in particular, because God has granted to you before all nations outstanding military glory, as we have already said. Therefore take this journey for the remission of your sins, certain of the unfading glory of the kingdom of heaven.

race absolutely alien to God . . . has invaded the land of those Christians, has reduced the people with sword, rapine [pillaging] and flame and has carried off some as captives to its own land, has cut down others by pitiable murder and has either completely razed churches of God to the ground or enslaved them to the practice of its own rites.[5]

Urban called for a Christian expedition to the Holy Land, especially Jerusalem, to fight against the Turks. He offered remission from sin—called an indulgence—as a reward to anyone who would take the cross (make a vow to go on crusade). He also guaranteed that all participants would receive a place in heaven. At a time when most Europeans felt that sin was inescapable, Urban was offering them the chance to start afresh. Urban's promise of an indulgence and an eternity in heaven were powerful motivators for people to join the crusade.

Urban's speech was followed by cries of *"Deus lo volt,"* or "God wills it" from the crowd, who surged forward to take the cross. Within a matter of months, various armies made up of knights, foot soldiers, nobles, peasants, and even clergy set out on what would become the First Crusade.

The First Crusade

Pope Urban's forces in the First Crusade (1096–1102) consisted of four major armies, each with a different leader and following a different route to Constantinople, their meeting point. The armies led by Robert of Flanders and Bohemond of Taranto traveled by sea from Italy, while those led by Godfrey of Bouillon and Raymond of Toulouse traveled by land. Smaller groups followed local lords or nobles, and some people went eastward on their own. Altogether, thousands of men, women, and children joined the crusade and made their way to Constantinople.

Most historians view only the First Crusade as having been successful in achieving its goals: capturing key cities in the Holy Land, including Antioch in 1098 and Jerusalem in 1099. The crusaders—

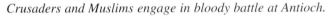

Crusaders and Muslims engage in bloody battle at Antioch.

who were called Franks by the Muslims and Latins by the Byzantines—also created western European–style settlements in the lands they conquered, complete with city walls and castles. These settlements were organized into the four kingdoms that were known as the crusader states, and they occupied most of the territory of present-day Israel, Lebanon, Jordan, and Syria.

Even though it achieved its objectives, the First Crusade still had many problems that would be typical of the failures of crusades to come. The pope had tried to limit those who went on crusade to able-bodied knights by discouraging the sick, elderly, women, children, clerics, and monks from taking the cross. Nonetheless, thousands of noncombatants—that is, people who were unarmed and took no part in the fighting—joined the crusade. Some knights took their entire families along. Problems of leadership and command, as well as loyalty, also arose. The First Crusade had no single, widely accepted leader, and the crusaders divided into factions that did not always get along. Also, no one agreed with Emperor Alexius over the fate of reconquered lands that had formerly been part of the Byzantine Empire. Nicaea in present-day Turkey was returned to the emperor, but the crusaders kept the land of the crusader states. This led to a great deal of tension and mistrust between the crusaders and their Byzantine allies, a situation that would continue to exist throughout the Crusades.

Failed Holy War

The primary objective of the Crusades was to win control of the Holy Land—particularly Jerusalem—from the Muslims. But there were other goals as well, among them defending the Byzantine Empire from the Turks, reuniting the Western and Eastern Churches, and diverting the warlike tendencies of the quarrelsome European rulers by giving them a common external enemy to fight against. When Urban preached to the crowd assembled at Clermont, he begged of those present, "Let those who once fought against brothers and relatives now rightfully fight against barbarians."[6]

Another objective of the Crusades was to establish and maintain Christian kingdoms in the Holy Land after the crusaders had conquered it. Holding on to the land around Jerusalem and the other holy places in Syria, Lebanon, and Palestine (roughly the area of present-day Israel) was crucial if the Christians hoped to keep the land out of the hands of the Muslims. Moreover, creating kingdoms in the Holy Land would give second and third sons of nobles, who had no hope for land of their own in Europe, a place to settle. Peasants who hoped to escape from poverty and famine were also eager to migrate to the legendary "land of milk and honey" spoken of in the Bible. Most Europeans had the idea that life would be better and easier in the East and that their settlements would be as opulent as the Byzantine cities they had heard about.

But this grand plan had several flaws, and many of these failings were evident even from the time of the First Crusade. The reasons for failure were diverse and included inadequate armies, an erosion of popular support for the crusading movement, the difficulties involved in conducting war in a faraway place, and an inability to defend the land the crusaders had conquered in the East. But it is just possible, as historian Steven Runciman suggests, that the Crusades failed because they were a folly from the start, born of intolerance and fed by greed:

> The Crusades were a tragic and destructive episode. The historian as he gazes back across the centuries at their gallant story must find his admiration overcast by sorrow at the witness that it bears to the limitations of human nature. There was so much courage and so little honour, so much devotion and so little understanding. High ideals were besmirched by cruelty and greed, enterprise and endurance by a blind and narrow self-righteousness; and the Holy War itself was nothing more than a long act of intolerance in the name of God. [7]

It required a combination of arrogance and overconfidence for the European Christians to believe that they could travel thousands of miles away to a foreign country, drive the native population out of cities and lands they had occupied for centuries, and impose their own government, religion, language, and civilization on those they believed were inferior to them because they were of a different religion. And while the crusaders might have won some initial successes, in the end the flaws in their grandiose plan would prevent the future generations of crusaders from realizing ultimate victory in the Holy Land.

The Doomed Armies of the Crusades

Chapter 2

CRUSADING ARMIES CONTAINED hundreds of knights who were well trained, well armed, and highly experienced in battle. But alongside these knights were thousands of peasants who lacked training, discipline, and skill at warfare. Throngs of peasants from all across Europe were attracted by the idea of having all their sins washed away, starting anew in the Holy Land, and being assured a place in heaven, and these people took up arms and went on crusade. The armies were also accompanied by noncombatants, including family members and support personnel who saw to the daily needs of the soldiers. Far from being an insignificant group, the noncombatants numbered in the thousands.

Of the entire fighting force that participated during the two centuries of the Crusades, only a small number were trained fighters. For example, less than 10 percent of the army of the First Crusade con-

Peasant crusaders, shown here, were often unarmed and lacked the skill and discipline necessary to succeed in battle.

sisted of knights. The vast majority who took part in the Church's holy war were peasants who had no formal training in warfare. To make matters worse, the crusaders were frequently in conflict about who was in command. A military such as this had little possibility of winning any war, let alone a war against a highly trained and experienced fighting force such as the Turkish Muslims.

Thousands of Noncombatants

Having so many people who were not knights or foot soldiers taking the cross hindered the Crusades. In some ways, this could not be helped. The knights and soldiers needed the assistance of cooks, grooms, servants, smiths, armorers, and church clerics to function. Though untrained in warfare, and in many cases unarmed, these noncombatants accompanied the crusading armies to the Holy Land. In addition, many knights and soldiers who did not want to leave their families behind during what was certain to be a long absence simply took their wives and children with them. Others who planned to settle in Jerusalem also brought their families along on crusade.

The large numbers of noncombatants—including women and children—who went along with the knights and foot soldiers created a multitude of problems. They depleted the crusaders' food supply and contributed to many famines, most notably at Antioch in Asia Minor. There, in 1098, a crusading army was trapped inside the walls of Antioch for nine months while the Muslims laid siege to the city. Raymond of Aguilers, a chaplain who was present, describes the hardships that the besieged crusaders suffered:

> There was such a famine in the city that the head of a horse without the tongue would be sold for two or three sous, the innards of a goat for five sous, a hen for eight or nine sous. As to bread I can only say that five sous would not be enough to offset the hunger of one person. Many knights lived on the blood of their horses, since in hope of God's mercy they did not want to kill them yet.[8]

The large number of noncombatants inside the city competed with the knights and soldiers for scraps from the dwindling food supply. During the famine, the army's effectiveness was hampered because the food that the the noncombatants consumed could have gone to the trained soldiers, who were more useful in battle than the

An Unclean Society

During the Middle Ages Europeans did not practice good personal hygiene. In their book *Life in a Medieval Village*, Frances and Joseph Gies write that medieval Europe was "a not very well washed society." Because they did not bathe often, the crusaders were susceptible to disease and plagues; in fact, King Louis IX died of the plague at Tunis in 1270 during the last crusade.

By contrast, Muslim society performed ceremonial bathing as part of their religious practice. According to William H. McNeill's book *Plagues and Peoples*, "Washing, whether in water or with sand, plays a prominent part in Moslem . . . ritual; and that, too, may sometimes have had the effect of checking the spread of infections." The Muslim prohibition on eating pork, which was seen as unclean because hogs were scavengers who ate human feces and other unclean material, helped prevent some parasitic infestations and so may have kept Muslims healthier than their Christian counterparts during the Crusades.

noncombatants were. It was not only the crusaders who suffered at Antioch, but also the cause for which they had made their difficult journey.

A Disorganized, Undisciplined Army

The lack of discipline and organization among the thousands of untrained peasants who took the cross represented another obstacle to success. One of the most disastrous examples of this problem came to be known as the People's Crusade, which was led by a French monk named Peter the Hermit. Although Peter's army contained several hundred knights and foot soldiers, it was made up primarily of thousands of unruly peasants of both sexes, including children and what one historian describes as "old people in rags."[9]

The pope had set August 15, 1096, as the official date for the four major armies of the First Crusade to depart. The armies planned to travel separately, by different routes, and meet in Constantinople before proceeding to the Holy Land. But Peter and his followers were too impatient to wait for the official departure date and left France in the spring of 1096. The ragtag members of the People's Crusade marched across Europe, gaining more followers as they went.

Shortly after Peter arrived outside the walls of Constantinople with his followers, the Byzantine emperor advised him to avoid the city of Nicaea, which was heavily fortified and defended by the Turks. But Peter was no longer in charge of the horde of peasants, who now decided to take matters into their own hands. They defied his order to wait for the official armies to arrive. Instead, Peter's mob of twenty thousand people sailed across the Bosporus Strait without him and marched headlong into Asia Minor to battle the Turks alone. Anna Comnena, the daughter of the Byzantine emperor, described the disaster that befell the rampaging peasant army:

> Without a moment's hesitation they set out on the Nicaea road in complete disorder, practically heedless of military discipline and the proper arrangement which should mark men going off to war. . . . They set out helter-skelter, regardless of their individual companies. Near the [village of] Drakon they fell into the Turkish [ambush] and were miserably slaughtered. So great a multitude of . . . Normans [crusaders] died by the Ishmaelite [Muslim] sword that when they gathered the remains of the fallen, lying on every side, they heaped up, I will not say a mighty ridge or hill or peak, but a mountain of considerable height and depth and width, so huge was the mass of bones. [10]

In her memoir Anna Comnena blames the disaster at Drakon on the uncontrolled behavior of Peter's followers, who apparently were following no one. They had defied his orders, abandoned their leader,

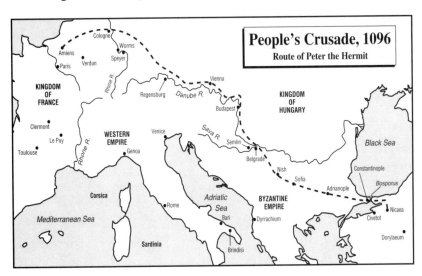

People's Crusade, 1096
Route of Peter the Hermit

and acted on their own initiative, ignoring the advice of the Byzantine emperor not to face the Turks without reinforcements. The disorganization and lack of discipline in the People's Crusade resulted in a slaughter that cost seventeen thousand lives.

The Children's Crusade

Undersupplied, disorganized, and untrained as they were, the crusaders stood little chance of victory against the Turks at almost every stage of their journey. No single event illustrates the futility of their efforts better, however, than the so-called Children's Crusade. In 1212, two groups of unarmed children from France and Germany set out for the Holy Land, believing they could recapture Jerusalem from the Muslims, even though they had no weapons.

The largest group, led by a twelve-year-old farm boy named Stephen of Cloyes, consisted of around thirty thousand children aged

The Children's Crusade, illustrated here, consisted of thousands of unarmed children who believed they could capture the Holy Land.

ten to eighteen. Stephen led them on foot across France from Vendôme to the port of Marseilles, where, according to one historian, "they expected the Lord to part the waters for them, as He had done for Moses, so that they could walk dry-shod across the Mediterranean to the Holy Land."[11]

The German group was led by ten-year-old Nicholas of Cologne. Most of the German children perished during the arduous journey across the Alps. According to historian Elizabeth Hallam, the survivors reached Italy, where, "weakened by hunger, and suffering from their long journey, some of the German boys sailed from Pisa, to an unknown fate."[12] The remainder of the group marched to France, where they joined Stephen's group at Marseilles.

None of the nearly fifty thousand participants in the Children's Crusade ever reached Jerusalem. Instead, they were lured aboard ships in Marseilles by traders promising them safe passage. Two of the ships sank en route, and the rest of the children were sold as slaves to the Muslims in northern Africa. While nobles and church officials may have known the children were doomed, they did nothing to stop them. In fact, Pope Innocent III praised the youthful crusaders by saying, "These children put us to shame, they rush to recover the Holy Land while we sleep."[13] Yet this army of children, led by children, had no chance of succeeding in gaining control of the Holy Land. Most of them did not even survive the journey across Europe. In fact, the only members of the Children's Crusade to face the Muslims at all did so as slaves.

A Lack of Clear Leadership

The lack of organization within the ranks of the crusaders was matched by the absence of a clear command structure at higher levels. On many occasions, one commander made decisions and gave orders that conflicted with the decisions and orders of other commanders. This problem was most apparent during the Fifth Crusade, which was led by the French king, John of Brienne.

The Fifth Crusade had sailed to the shores of Egypt in 1218 in hopes of capturing Muslim ports there. The crusaders saw the Egyptian ports as bargaining chips for gaining territory in the Holy Land, and in the thirteenth century Egypt was the destination of several crusades. In August of 1218 the crusaders under John of Brienne captured the Chain Tower at Damietta, a strategic port city at the mouth of the Nile delta. The Chain Tower was on the opposite bank of the Nile from the city and was used for stringing a huge chain across the river as a barrier to naval attack. From the tower, the crusaders launched the siege of Damietta.

An expedition under Cardinal Pelagius arrived in September to help in the attack. Pelagius had been sent to Egypt as the official representative of the pope. Pelagius saw the crusaders as being under Church jurisdiction and refused to accept the leadership of John. Pelagius wanted to be in charge of the crusade, and his interference often resulted in unwise military decisions. For example, in February 1219, the Muslims offered peace terms, including cession of Jerusalem to the crusaders. John and the European barons advised acceptance, but Pelagius refused because he thought it was wrong to come to terms with infidels (non-Christians). The siege continued until the following November, when the crusaders finally took Damietta after eighteen months.

After the victory at Damietta, the tensions between John and Pelagius did not subside, and John finally left Egypt. The crusading army was left without its chief commander, and they remained at a standstill for the next twenty months, refusing to follow the orders of Pelagius because they did not see him as their leader. While the crusaders awaited a new commander, the Egyptian sultan foritified his garrison at nearby El Mansûra.

Meanwhile, the pope ordered John to return to the crusade in Egypt. In August 1221, a month after John's return, the crusading army advanced down the east bank of the Nile. John had argued with Pelagius against the march because the Nile was flooding, but he finally gave in to Pelagius's insistence. The crusading army marched to a narrow strip of land between two branches of the river and stopped on the bank opposite El Mansûra. The sultan blocked the river route between the crusaders and Damietta, which not only cut off the crusaders' supply line but also blocked the way back to their garrison at Damietta. The crusaders were forced to retreat. However, the Muslims had sent troops to block the crusaders' retreat. Oliver of Paderborn, the secretary to Cardinal Pelagius, described the discord among the crusading army that was trapped along the banks of the flooding Nile River:

Franks attack the Muslim city of Damietta during the Fifth Crusade.

From the day on which we lost control of the river, our coun-
selors met frequently to discuss whether it would be more ex-
pedient to stay in the camp and await the galleys [ships]
which had been promised by the emperor, Frederick II, or to
make a sortie [attack] at whatever cost, in view of the shortage of supplies. The majority was in favour of a sortie, which
was rather dangerous because of the approach of the enemy
and because the flood-waters would certainly constitute an
obstruction. But one from the humbler ranks . . . gave it as his
opinion that we should await reinforcements within our forti-
fications . . . since our supplies would still last, if carefully
rationed, for twenty days. This advice was not, however, accepted, and it was decided instead to make a sortie by night.[14]

The sortie over which there had been so much disagreement
proved to be the final defeat of the army of the Fifth Crusade. Oliver
of Paderborn goes on to describe the lack of leadership that contributed to the disaster at El Mansûra:

Our disastrous situation was exacerbated by the fact that the men were mostly drunk that night with wine. . . ; they were now left behind asleep in the camp or lay in the road and could not be roused, and were for the most part slaughtered or captured and so lost to us. Others plunged into the flood-waters in the darkness of the night and were left struggling helplessly in the deep mud. Still others fell upon the boats, and weighed them down so much that they sank. On the same night we lost the camels and mules bearing burdens of silver vessels, clothes and tents and, more injuriously, arrows for our defense. The Templars [a military religious order that fought in the crusades] led the rearguard, in the greatest peril, keeping well together with their weapons held in readi-ness to protect those who were marching ahead of them. But the men in front headed off in different directions and wan-dered through the dark night like stray sheep.[15]

The faltering army of the Fifth Crusade, nearly leaderless and ham-pered by thousands of noncombatants, was out-fought by the well-trained and well-led Muslim army. Throughout the two hundred years of warfare in the Holy Land, the Christian armies had to face opponents whose skill and experience in warfare outweighed their own.

A Formidable Foe

The Muslim armies were quite capable of defending their home-lands. Their warriors were mostly Seljuq Turks, a nomadic tribe orig-inally from the steppes of central Asia. The Turks had migrated southwestward in the eleventh century and had swiftly overrun much of Asia Minor, including Persia, Armenia, Iraq, and many Byzantine provinces. They were fierce warriors who had a long history of con-quest, and they inspired fear and awe in their opponents.

The crusading forces were made up of many individual armies from different lands, speaking different languages. These armies were simply thrown together and transported fifteen hundred miles to fight an enemy force that was designed for conquest. European armies were developed primarily to fight other European armies that fought just like themselves, with the same equipment and tactics, and, perhaps most important, were also located in Europe. But the Muslims—especially the Turks—had learned to adapt to defeat a wide variety of opponents in different locales. Also, the Turks were perhaps more motivated to defend their homelands than the crusaders were to conquer them, because the crusaders knew they could always go back to Europe. Finally, because the Turks were on their own territory, they knew the land and how to survive there. Thus, even when the crusaders captured territory, the Turks were able to withdraw, regroup, and attack the Frankish settlements from secure bases.

The Turks' skills as horsemen and archers were legendary. Historian Elizabeth Hallam says, "A knowledge of the theories of horsemanship and archery, combined with regular training, enabled the

Turkish warriors, who were skilled horsemen and archers, defend their territory in the Second Crusade.

Knights on horseback charge defenders who have their spears ready during one of the many battles of the Crusades.

Turks to develop such dexterity that they could shoot from horseback without slowing, and turn in the saddle to fire when in retreat."[16] The Turks used their skills at horsemanship when facing the attacking crusaders and developed superior tactics to deal with the knights' cavalry charge.

The Cavalry Charge

The crusaders' most common method of fighting their opponents in the field was the cavalry charge, in which the entire army would attack in one large formation. The more experienced warriors would lead the charge on horseback, armed with swords. They were followed by mounted archers and the more prominent lords and knights, who were armed with lances. The formation began its advance on the enemy at a walk, proceeded to a trot when they were a few hundred yards from the enemy, then charged the last seventy-five yards at a gallop. The success of the cavalry charge depended on the knights remaining organized in their formation, and when efficiently employed it could have a devastating effect on their opponents. Cavalry charges were usually followed by bloody hand-to-hand combat with spears, swords, lances, and daggers.

When it came to hand-to-hand combat, the opposing sides were similarly armed with axes, pikes, lances, and swords. However, the knights wore chain-mail armor for protection in battle. Chain mail consisted of a tunic that was made of linked metal rings and that covered the body from neck to knee. As the Crusades progressed, improved weaponry that could penetrate older forms of armor made it necessary for knights to wear stronger, heavier forms of plate armor for protection. This armor gave them the advantage in hand-to-hand combat because they had more protection than the Turks, who wore less armor. But the knights' heavy armor put them at a disadvantage in the cavalry charge. Because they were weighed down by as much as sixty pounds of armor, they needed horses that were large and strong, though not necessarily fast. The Turks, who wore less armor, were able to use lighter, faster horses, which gave them the advantage of speed and mobility over the heavily armored knights. And because Turks knew the crusaders' armor protected them during hand-to-hand combat, they tried to disable and disconcert the crusaders as much as possible during the cavalry charge.

The Superior Tactics of the Turks

The Turks who faced these cavalry charges were not organized into a single formation, as the crusaders were. Rather, they formed many

 Admiration for the Turks's Skill in Warfare

The crusaders held many false ideas about Muslims—among them that they worshiped idols, prayed to many gods, and were less than human. Despite these prejudices, the crusaders who fought against the Muslim Turks in the First Crusade were so impressed by their fighting skill that, according to historian Marcus Bull in *The Oxford History of the Crusades*, edited by Jonathan Riley-Smith,

> [The crusaders] speculated whether their adversaries might in fact be distant relatives, a sort of lost tribe which centuries before had been diverted from its migration towards Europe and Christian civilization. This was no idle compliment in an age when character traits were believed to be transmitted by blood and stories about the descent of peoples from biblical or mythical forebears went to the very heart of Europeans' sense of historical identity and communal worth.

small groups to encircle the knights. The Turks preceded their attacks by making a great din with trumpets, drums, and cymbals to frighten their opponents. Historian Carole Hillenbrand explains that "they would come charging at full speed towards the enemy and then at the last moment wheel round and shoot as they retreated."[17] The Turks would fire a volley of arrows at the charging knights. Although the arrows did not seriously injure the heavily armored crusaders, they did cause the knights to scatter in different directions and left them in a state of confusion and disarray. If the Turks were able to break up the solid formation of charging crusaders, they could then surround the smaller groups. Thus, as the knights' composure and strict formation broke down, they became more vulnerable to attack.

Knights use swords, axes, and other weapons to fight battles on horseback.

Political Rivalry in the Third Crusade

The problem of European rulers fighting among themselves was perhaps most apparent during the Third Crusade, led by Philip II Augustus of France and Richard I Lionheart of England. Philip and Richard argued over how the battles should be fought and who was in charge of the crusade. These two men, who considered themselves to be enemies, agreed to be joint leaders of a crusade precisely because they did not trust each other. Richard ruled England and half of France, while Philip wanted the English holdings in France for his own. The two men feared that if either of them went on crusade without the other, he risked having his lands attacked by the other.

Many medieval European nobles and chroniclers believed that this bitter rivalry between Philip and Richard undermined their ability to cooperate during the Third Crusade and ultimately hampered its success. The conflicts began even before the two crusading armies reached the Holy Land. Richard's army had captured and sacked the town of Messina in Sicily and divided the spoils among themselves. Philip demanded to share the credit for Richard's capture of Messina—as well as the spoils—but Richard refused, and this event sparked a feud that clouded the rest of the crusade. Later, when Richard captured the island of Cyprus, Philip also demanded, and was refused, control of half of the island.

After an argument with Richard over the rightful succession to the throne of the kingdom of Jerusalem, Philip, who was ill, frustrated, and angry with Richard, returned to France. There, he began plotting to overthrow Richard with the help of Richard's younger brother, John.

During the negotiations over Jerusalem with the Muslim leader Saladin, Richard was distracted by the troubles back home: Not only was his brother trying to usurp him as king, Philip had also invaded Richard's lands in France despite their pact to protect each other's lands during the crusade. Richard was also commanding a divided force—his knights did not trust the French knights, and the French knights did not trust him. The final result of the Third Crusade was that, although Richard signed a treaty with Saladin allowing Christian pilgrims access to the holy sites in Jerusalem, he failed to take the city from the Muslims.

As the initial wave of Turkish archers retreated, another would charge in to take its place, fire another volley of arrows into the knights' disintegrating formation, and then retreat briskly. The Turks employed these hit-and-run tactics repeatedly to disrupt the crusaders as much as possible before the close combat began. In this way, the Turks were often able to gain the advantage and emerge victorious on the battlefield.

This passage from the early thirteenth-century book *Itinerarium regis Ricardi* (*The Travels of King Richard*), which is based on eye-witness accounts, describes how the hit-and-run fighting tactics of the Turks helped defeat the army of King Richard I of England during the Third Crusade:

> The Turks, unlike our men, are not weighed down with ar-mour, so they are able to advance more rapidly, and often in-flict serious damage on our forces. . . . When forcibly driven off they flee on very swift horses, the fastest in the world, like swallows for speed. Also they have this trick of halting their flight when they see that their pursuers have given up the chase. An irritating fly, if you drive it off, will leave you, but when you desist, it returns. As long as you go on swat-ting it, it keeps off, once you stop, back it comes. This is just like the Turk—when you give up the pursuit and turn back, then he comes after you, but if you drive him off again, he will take flight. So while King Richard kept up the chase they fled, but when he turned back they threatened his rear, not always with impunity, but often inflicting severe losses on our men.[18]

The unprepared, unskilled, and divided military that waged the Crusades practically ensured failure in this holy war. Though they captured a large area in the Holy Land during the First Crusade, the crusaders were attempting a military feat that was clearly impossible. As more and more people in Europe became discouraged by the cru-saders' defeats and the questionable tactics they often used, popular support for the Crusades began to wane.

A Loss of
Chapter 3 Popular Support

THE CRUSADES WERE a mass movement involving hundreds of thousands of people over a period of two centuries. Popular support in Europe was important to the crusading effort because the armies were made up largely of volunteers from the general population. Without the participation of the masses of people who made a vow to fight the Muslims in the Holy Land, the Crusades would not have taken place at all.

At the start of the Crusades, popular support in Europe was high. People who took the cross during the First Crusade were venerated, and families were still proud of their crusading ancestors two to three generations later. But by the beginning of the thirteenth century, popular support for the Crusades began to fade. Although there were many reasons for this change, one of the key factors was the barbarity of the crusaders.

Crusading armies committed numerous atrocities throughout the Crusades, including massacres of Jewish and Muslim men, women, and children and the destruction and looting of cities they conquered. A turning point was reached in 1204 when the crusaders attacked Constantinople, murdering its inhabitants and razing its buildings. Constantinople was a Christian city and the capital of the Byzantine Empire, and therefore a city the crusaders had sworn to help defend. While Europeans may have been willing to tolerate massacres of Jews and Muslims, whom they saw as the enemies of Christ, they drew the line at massacres of fellow Christians.

The excessive and indiscriminate violence of the crusaders led the public to question whether it was right to fight wars in the name of religion. These doubts over the morality of the Crusades ultimately

A fervent believer rallies support for his cause despite waning public interest.

contributed to a decline in popular support for the Church's holy war. The enthusiasm that earlier crusaders displayed gradually faded, and people became more wary of taking the cross. Because fewer and fewer people took the cross, later crusading armies were much smaller. In contrast to the sixty thousand to one hundred thousand members of the combined armies of the First Crusade, the army of the Seventh Crusade numbered only fifteen thousand. The crusaders could not continue to wage battle against the Muslims to defend Christian possessions or to regain lost territory with such a small army. The loss of popular support that resulted from the excessive brutality of the Crusades represented yet another fatal blow to the crusading movement.

A Violent Culture

Although the Crusades were a series of holy wars fought mainly for a religious cause, they were wars nonetheless. Violence was an expected part of any war and was acceptable to the public at the beginning of the crusading movement. In fact, violence was so common in eleventh-century Europe that it was considered a normal part of everyday life. For example, legal disputes were commonly resolved through battles, and convicted felons were often mutilated or put to death, even for offenses such as theft. According to noted historian Jonathan Riley-Smith,

Brutality was so common it could be ritualistic. In about 1100, for example, a knight from Gascony prayed at the monastery of Sorde that God would enable him to catch his brother's murderer. The intended victim was ambushed, his face was horribly mutilated, his hands and feet were cut off, and he was castrated. In this way his prestige, his capacity to fight, and his dynastic prospects were all irreparably damaged. Moved by feelings of gratitude for what he believed had been divine assistance, the avenging knight presented his enemy's bloodstained armour and weapons as a pious offering to the monks of Sorde. These they accepted.[19]

Like other institutions of medieval Europe, the Church accepted violence as a natural part of life. At the beginning of the crusading movement, a certain amount of violence and savagery did not seem out of place. This way of thinking helps explain the overall lack of concern about massacres of non-Christians during the early years of the Crusades.

Massacres of Jews

Jews and Muslims were both targets of the crusaders—the Muslims because they had taken control of Jerusalem and other cities that were holy to the Christians, and the Jews because they were considered responsible for the death of Christ. In 1096 and 1097 the Jewish inhabitants of several towns in the Rhineland in present-day Germany were massacred by the People's Crusade as it moved through Europe on its way to Constantinople. These followers of Peter the Hermit wondered why they should travel all the way to the Holy Land to fight the so-called enemies of God when there were Jews living nearby in Europe. The crusaders forced Jews to be baptized and perpetrated horrifying massacres of Jews in several towns, including Worms, Mainz, Cologne, Trier, and Metz. The medieval German chronicler Albert of Aachen described the slaughter of the Jews in Cologne in 1096:

> They suddenly attacked a small band of Jews, they decapitated many and inflicted serious wounds, they destroyed their homes and synagogues, and divided a very great sum of looted money among themselves.
>
> When the Jews saw this cruelty, about two hundred started to flee by boat to Neuss in the stillness of the night; but the pilgrims

and crusaders discovered them and did not leave a single one alive. Moreover, after they had massacred them all, they robbed them of all their possessions.[20]

This sort of violence against Jews was repeated many times during the Crusades. In the Second Crusade, groups in northern France and the Rhineland followed the example set by the People's Crusade, murdering and pillaging in towns where Jews lived. Perhaps one of the most horrible examples of a massacre of innocent people during the Crusades happened in Jerusalem in 1099, when the victorious crusaders sacked the city and slaughtered all the Jewish and Muslim inhabitants.

The Sack of Jerusalem

The crusaders commonly followed the capture of a Muslim city by sacking it—killing the citizens, destroying mosques and other holy buildings, and looting treasures. The crusaders captured Jerusalem from the Muslims in July 1099 after besieging the city for more than a month. During the week of chaos that followed, the city's Muslim and Jewish populations—perhaps as many as seventy thousand people—were massacred. Muslim author Amin Maalouf describes the crusaders as "heavily armoured warriors spilling through the streets, swords in hand, slaughtering men, women, and children, plundering houses, sacking mosques." Those Muslims who survived the slaughter had a hideous task forced upon them: "to heave the bodies of their own relatives, to dump them in vacant, unmarked lots, and then to set them alight, before being themselves massacred or sold into slavery." [21]

Maalouf describes the fate of the Jews of Jerusalem as "no less atrocious" than that of the Muslims. After the first few hours of battle, in which the Jews had defended their quarter of the city, the crusaders broke through the city walls and began streaming into the streets. The sight caused the Jews to panic, and "the entire community gathered in the main synagogue to pray. The [Franks] barricaded all the exits and stacked all the bundles of wood they could find in a ring around the building. The temple was then put to the torch. Those who managed to escape were massacred in the neighbouring alleyways. The rest were burned alive."[22]

But the atrocities that the crusaders committed in Jerusalem did not stop with the massacre of the city's Muslim and Jewish inhabitants. The crusaders went on to ravage the very city they claimed to venerate

Crusaders use a catapult as one of their many weapons in laying siege to the city of Jerusalem.

and had come to liberate. A Norman knight named Tancred and his men looted the Dome of the Rock, a sacred Muslim shrine. The Dome of the Rock is built around the Foundation Stone, on which Abraham is said to have offered his son as a sacrifice to God and from which Muhammad (the founder of Islam) is said to have visited heaven. According to Ibn al-Athir, an Arab historian who was an eyewitness to the Crusades, "The Franks stripped the Dome of the Rock of more than forty silver candelabra, each of them weighing 3,600 drams [thirty-seven pounds], and a great silver lamp weighing forty-four Syrian pounds, as well as a hundred and fifty smaller silver candelabra and more than twenty gold ones, and a great deal more booty."[23]

Although many people in Europe were upset by the destruction and looting of this holiest of cities, they accepted it as a necessary evil to capture Jerusalem from the Muslims, who had held the city for nearly five centuries. Although killing was considered a sin that required an act of penance to gain forgiveness, the slaughter of the city's inhabitants was more or less tolerated by European Christians because Jews and Muslims were considered infidels. Killing these so-called enemies of Christ was seen as morally justifiable and did not require penance—in fact, killing to defend Christendom was actually a penance in itself. More-over, Europeans considered violence committed during the Crusades to be right and morally justifiable because the Crusades were a holy war sanctioned by the pope and thus, they believed, by God.

Cannibalism at Ma'arra

Even though Pope Urban had sanctioned violence against the Muslims in the form of a holy war, he did not approve of all the crusaders' actions. In 1098, for example, the crusaders laid siege to Ma'arra, to the north-west of Antioch in present-day Turkey. There are numerous accounts by medieval chroni-clers of the Crusades about acts of cannibalism committed by the crusaders at Ma'arra. After two weeks of fighting, the city surrendered, and when the crusaders entered the city they indulged in the customary three days of looting and slaughter. The Frankish chron-icler Radulf of Caen wrote that in Ma'arra "our troops boiled pagan adults in cooking pots; they impaled children on spits and devoured them grilled."[24]

Pope Urban II, head of the Church during the First Crusade.

The pope was willing to tolerate killing Turks because they were Muslim and there-fore enemies of the Church. And following a victory with three days of pillage and slaughter was common practice during the Middle Ages and therefore not out of the ordinary. But Urban was horrified by the accounts he received of the crusaders' cannibalism and feared such barbarity might erode popular support for the crusading effort. The commander of the crusading army at Ma'arra wrote a letter to explain the episode to the pope, justifying the actions of his forces by claiming they were driven to such an extreme only because of ram-pant starvation due to a shortage of supplies.

The Great City of Constantinople

In time, stories of the brutality perpetrated by the crusaders on innocent people did, as Pope Urban had feared, begin to erode popular support in Europe. While many events contributed to the loss of popular support, none did as much damage to the Crusades as the siege and sack of Constantinople, the capital of the Byzantine Empire.

During the Middle Ages, Constantinople was the world's largest and richest city. No European cities could compare to it. The populations of London and Paris were about 10,000 each, and Rome had a population of perhaps 30,000. But the population of Constantinople was at least 250,000. The city spread over seven hills covering an area of many square miles. It was protected by a massive double-wall system that was four miles long with towers every sixty yards. Beyond the double walls was a moat about thirty feet deep and sixty feet wide. This triple defensive system was legendary in the medieval world and had kept the city safe from invasion for eight hundred years. The Byzantine Empire had defended Christendom against invasion from the East for centuries.

Constantinople, pictured here, was the largest and richest city in the world during the Middle Ages.

The Looting of Constantinople's Churches

In 1204, the Christian crusaders who had been sent to defend the
Byzantine Empire against the Turks attacked the Byzantine capital of
Constantinople and laid waste to its treasures. The following account
of the sack of Constantinople, from a late medieval Russian narrative
known as *The Chronicle of Novgorod*, is reprinted in *Chronicles of the
Crusades: Eye-Witness Accounts of the Wars between Christianity and
Islam*, edited by Elizabeth Hallam:

> All the Franks entered the town [Constantinople] on Monday 12
> April [1204], and stopped at the place where the Greek emperor
> had stood, by St Saviour's, and stayed there for the night. Next
> morning at sunrise they went into the church of Hagia Sophia
> and tore down the doors, and cut them to pieces, and the pulpit
> cased in silver, and twelve silver pillars, and four pillars of the icon
> case. They cut up the icon bracket and twelve crosses which
> hung over the altar with bosses between them, like trees taller
> than a man, and the altar rails between the pillars, which was all
> silver. They tore the precious stone and the great pearl from the
> marvelous altar, and where they put the altar itself is not known.
>
> They took forty large cups which were in front of the altar, and
> the censers [incense burners] and the silver lamps, whose num-
> ber we cannot tell, with priceless feast-day dishes. The gospels
> for the services and the holy crosses, priceless icons, all this they
> stripped. Under the altar roof they found forty barrels of pure
> gold, in shelves in the walls and in the places where dishes are
> kept, an unheard-of quantity of gold and silver, so great as to be
> uncountable, and of priceless vessels. All this was in Hagia Sophia
> alone; but they also stripped the Holy Mother of God in Blach-
> ernae, where the Holy Spirit comes down every Friday. About
> the other churches man cannot tell, as they were countless.

Within Constantinople's city walls were luxurious palaces and
huge, domed churches. The city's churches contained relics from the
Holy Land, including a lock of hair from John the Baptist, the Crown
of Thorns presumed to have been worn by Christ, and a piece of
wood presumed to be from the cross on which Christ died. Besides
being the capital of the Byzantine Empire, and therefore an important ally to the crusading forces, Constantinople was also the center
of the Orthodox Church. It was therefore considered a holy city, often called the "New Rome," and its splendid collection of holy relics
made it almost as popular a destination for Christian pilgrims as
Jerusalem.

European visitors to this grand and luxurious city were often in awe of what they saw. The Frenchman Geoffrey of Villehardouin, who wrote a history of the Fourth Crusade, described the impression Constantinople made on him and his fellow crusaders when they arrived by ship in 1203:

> I can assure you that all those who had never seen Constantinople before gazed very intently at the city, having never imagined there could be so fine a place in the world. They noted the high walls and lofty towers encircling it, and its rich palaces and tall churches, of which there were so many that no one would have believed it to be true if he had not seen it with his own eyes, and viewed the length and breadth of that city which reigns supreme over all others. There was indeed no man so brave and daring that his flesh did not shudder at the sight. Nor was this to be wondered at, for never before had so grand an enterprise been carried out by any people since the creation of the world.[25]

The Sack of Constantinople

The siege and sack of the grand city of Constantinople during the ill-fated Fourth Crusade represented one of the greatest blunders of the Crusades. It destroyed the Church's most important ally in the East and signaled a turning point in the decline of popular support in Europe. The crusaders were supposed to help defend the Byzantine Empire, but instead they attacked and destroyed its capital city. The Byzantine Empire had defended Christendom against invasion from the East for centuries, but the attack on Constantinople by the army of the Fourth Crusade left the empire damaged beyond repair and more vulnerable than ever to invasion by the Turks.

The initial destination of the Fourth Crusade was Egypt, but the crusaders never reached Egypt and never fought against the Muslims. The crusade was diverted from its original goal because of financial reasons. The leaders of the crusade had made an agreement with merchants in Venice, who controlled finance, commerce, trade, and sea travel in the Mediterranean region, to provide ships to transport the crusading army to Egypt. But the crusade leaders had vastly overestimated the number of troops that would be in need of shipping.

Only 11,000 crusaders arrived in Venice, far short of the anticipated 33,500. The Venetians still expected to be paid in full, even for the ships the crusaders did not need. To pay the Venetians' bill, each crusader would have had to pay three times what he had expected, and though the leaders collected what they could, the crusaders still found themselves thirty-four thousand silver marks short. The Venetians persuaded the crusaders to attack the Venetians' rival, the trading port of Zara in present-day Croatia, and divide the spoils to pay their debt. The combined force captured and sacked Zara in 1202. The pope was enraged and excommunicated all the participants, meaning they could no longer enjoy the rights of church membership.

Constantinople residents cower before their conquerors. Crusaders sacked the city they had vowed to help defend.

The sack of Zara, a Christian city, was shocking enough in itself, but then the Venetians persuaded the crusaders to attack Constantinople, the world's richest city. Part of the motive for attacking was greed on the part of the Venetians, who wanted to eliminate their Byzantine trading rivals. But there was also greed on the part of the crusaders, who wanted this great city for themselves.

Robert of Clari, a French knight who participated in the Fourth Crusade, described the siege of Constantinople:

> On Monday 12 April 1204, in the morning, all the pilgrims [crusaders] and Venetians equipped and armed themselves fully. The Venetians repaired the assault bridges high in the masts of their ships; then they lined up ships, galleys and transports side by side and set off to the attack. The line of the fleet stretched out over more than three miles. When they neared the shore and were as close as they could get to the city walls, they dropped anchor. Then they mounted a furious artillery attack, bombarding the walls and hurling missiles and Greek fire [incendiary devices] at the towers, but these were all covered by leather hides and the fire did not take hold. The city's defenders fought fiercely. They had more than sixty stone-throwing siege-engines [catapults] and every time these were fired, missiles hit the ships, but the vessels were so well protected by timber planking and interwoven springy vines that the rocks did not do much damage, although each one was so big that one man could not have picked it up on his own.
>
> . . . The city's towers were so high that in all the Latin [crusader] fleet there were only four or five ships tall enough to be able to attack them.
>
> On top of the stone towers the Greeks had built wooden towers—up to five, six or sometimes seven storeys high—and these were manned by soldiers who defended them.
>
> The pilgrims kept up the attack until, by God's miracle, the sea, which is never calm there, carried the bishop of Soissons'

ship forward against one of these towers. A Venetian and two armed knights were perched high on the assault bridge of this ship. In the swell the ship swayed against the tower; the Venetian grabbed hold of the tower, clinging on with fingers and toes, and scrambled inside.[26]

The Alexiad of Anna Comnena

The sack of Constantinople in 1204 was not the first time the crusaders had shown aggression toward the Byzantine capital. In 1097 an army of the First Crusade launched a brief attack against Constantinople. In the following excerpt from her memoir, *The Alexiad of Anna Comnena*, Anna, daughter of the Byzantine emperor Alexius I Comnenus, describes the brief attack against Constantinople. The Byzantines were upset that the crusaders, who had come to defend them, would besiege the city, but even more disturbing to Anna was the fact that they attacked during Holy Week. Anna's father counseled restraint on the part of his generals. According to Anna,

> In the first place he insisted that no one whatever should leave the ramparts to attack the Latins [crusaders], for two reasons: because of the sacred character of the day (it was the Thursday of Holy Week, the supreme week of the year, in which the Saviour suffered an ignominious death on behalf of the whole world); and secondly because he wished to avoid bloodshed between Christians. On several occasions he sent envoys to the Latins advising them to desist from such an undertaking. "Have reverence," he said, "for God on this day was sacrificed for us all, refusing neither the Cross, nor the Nails, nor the Spear—proper instruments of punishment for evil-doers—to save us. If you must fight, we too shall be ready, but after the day of the Saviour's resurrection." They, far from listening to his words, rather reinforced their ranks, and so thick were the showers of their arrows that even one of the emperor's retinue, standing near the throne, was struck in the chest. Most of the others ranged on either side of the emperor, when they saw this, began to withdraw, but he remained seated and unruffled. . . . However, as he saw the Latins brazenly approaching the walls and rejecting sound advice, he took active steps for the first time. His son-in-law Nicephorous . . . was summoned. He was ordered to pick out the best fighters, expert archers, and post them on the ramparts; they were to fire volleys of arrows at the Latins, but without taking aim and mostly off-target, so as to terrify the enemy by the weight of the attack, but at all costs to avoid killing them. As I have remarked, he was fearful of desecrating that day and he wished to prevent fratricide.

The rest of the crusaders followed the Venetian's example and leaped from their ships' masts on to the towers. Ladders were affixed to other towers, and within a short time the city walls of Constantinople were breached. As the army of the Fourth Crusade swarmed through the streets of Constantinople, the emperor fled, followed by the city's defenders. By morning Constantinople had fallen to the crusaders. The besiegers then sacked the city for three days, murdering, raping, looting, and destroying. Wounded women and children were left to die in the streets during the pillage. According to noted historian John Julius Norwich, "Never since the barbarian invasions had Europe witnessed such an orgy of brutality and vandalism; never in history had so much beauty, so much superb craftsmanship, been wantonly destroyed in so short a space of time."[27]

In the frenzied scramble for booty, the crusaders smashed treasures and tore the city to pieces. The Venetians sent everything they could back to Venice, including four bronze horses that today still reside above the main door of St. Mark's Cathedral in Venice. In addition to looting, the crusaders also desecrated holy places, such as the sixth-century church of St. Sophia. The Byzantine historian Nicetas Choniates, who witnessed the carnage, wrote:

> They smashed the holy images and hurled the sacred relics of the Martyrs into places I am ashamed to mention, scattering everywhere the body and blood of the Saviour. . . . As for their profanation of the Great Church [St. Sophia], they destroyed the high altar and shared out the pieces among themselves. . . . And they brought horses and mules into the Church, the better to carry off the holy vessels, and the pulpit, and the doors, and the furniture wherever it was to be found; and when some of these beasts slipped and fell, they ran them through with their swords, fouling the Church with their blood and ordure [excrement].

> A common harlot was enthroned in the Patriarch's chair, to hurl insults at Jesus Christ; and she sang bawdy songs, and danced immodestly in the holy place . . . nor was there mercy shown to virtuous matrons, innocent maids or even virgins consecrated to God.[28]

The Consequences of the Fourth Crusade

Few people in Europe immediately understood what had occurred in Constantinople. At first, the relics that arrived in the churches of Europe were welcomed enthusiastically. But as detailed reports about

Arabic Chivalry

In many instances during the crusades, Arabic chivalry outshone that of the Europeans. The great twelfth-century Muslim leader Saladin is considered by Muslims and Europeans alike to be the embodiment of Arabic chivalry. In 1187, after Saladin recaptured Jerusalem, rather than massacring all the inhabitants—as the crusaders had done when they had taken the city in 1099—he allowed them all to be ransomed and released them without harm. This generosity helped inspire Saladin's reputation for chivalry. In his book *A History of the Crusades: The Kingdom of Jerusalem and the Frankish East, 1100–1187*, historian Steven Runciman describes Saladin's actions after recapturing Jerusalem:

The Muslim leader Saladin, shown here, raises his arms in victory.

The victors were correct and humane. Where the Franks, eighty-eight years before, had waded through the blood of their victims, not a building now was looted, not a person injured. By Saladin's orders guards patrolled the streets and the gates, preventing any outrage on the Christians. . . . Then Saladin himself announced that he would liberate every aged man and woman. When the Frankish ladies who had ransomed themselves came in tears to ask him where they should go, for their husbands or fathers were slain or captive, he answered by promising to release every captive husband, and to the widows and orphans he gave gifts from his own treasury, to each according to her estate. His mercy and kindness were in strange contrast to the deeds of the Christian conquerors of the First Crusade.

Knights, like the one pictured, were expected to be chivalrous at all times.

the brutal sack of the city reached Europe, this initial enthusiasm turned into misgivings. The crusaders in Constantinople had not behaved within the bounds of chivalry, the code of behavior that medieval knights were supposed to follow. Knights were expected to be polite, fair, noble, courageous, and, above all, good warriors. They were also supposed to show courtesy toward women, treat their fellow knights with respect, and follow certain rules of war such as not

Reuniting the Eastern and Western Churches

One of the goals of Pope Urban II and his successors was for the papacy to be in charge of a single, reunited Christian Church. After the crusaders captured Constantinople in 1204, Pope Innocent III hoped that the goal of reuniting the two branches of Christendom could now be attained. But he worried that the brutal way in which the Eastern Empire and Church had been subordinated to the West would not enable the situation to last. He was also upset to learn that the crusaders had established a new church organization in Constantinople—with the Venetians appointing a Latin patriarch—without any reference to him. Ultimately, by sacking Constantinople, the crusaders actually widened the rift between the Eastern and Western Churches, and thereby failed in one of the Crusades' chief goals. According to Steven Runciman's *A History of the Crusades: The Kingdom of Acre and the Later Crusades,*

> their barbarity left a memory that would never be forgiven them. Later, East Christian potentates might advocate union with Rome in the fond expectation that union would bring a united front against the Turks. But their people would not follow them. They could not forget the Fourth Crusade. It was perhaps inevitable that the Church of Rome and the great Eastern Churches should drift apart; but the whole Crusading movement had embittered their relations, and henceforward, whatever a few princes might try to achieve, in the hearts of the East Christians the schism was complete, irremediable and final.

attacking the unarmed. But in Constantinople the crusaders had violated the chivalric code that they were expected to uphold. Sacred buildings had been plundered, and fellow Christians had been murdered. The pope was appalled by the slaughter and the crusaders' barbarity, and he wrote to Constantinople to denounce the atrocities.

The destruction and desecration of Constantinople and the murder of thousands of its inhabitants led to the downfall of one of the world's greatest empires. The crusaders held Constantinople for nearly sixty years, turning it into another crusader state. The Byzantine Empire relocated its capital to Nicaea in present-day Turkey, and finally recaptured Constantinople from the crusaders in 1261. But it was too late; the destruction and looting of their richest city in 1204 left the Byzantine Empire permanently weakened. According to Norwich:

By the sack of Constantinople, Western civilization suffered a loss greater than the sack of Rome in the fifth century or the burning of the library of Alexandria in the seventh—perhaps the most catastrophic single loss in all history. Politically, too, the damage done was incalculable. Byzantium never recovered any considerable part of its lost dominion. Instead, the Empire was left powerless to defend itself against the [Muslim] Ottoman tide. There are few greater ironies in history than the fact that the fate of Eastern Christendom should have been sealed by men who fought under the banner of the Cross.[29]

In the end, the only aim of the Fourth Crusade was to conquer the territory of other Christians. People in Europe were upset by this fact and were ashamed of the crusaders' actions in Constantinople. The resulting erosion of popular support in the decades following the Fourth Crusade helped seal the fate of the crusading movement. Although four more major crusades would be launched over the next seventy years, popular support continued to fade, and without it the Crusades could not succeed. The consequences of the crusaders' conduct during the Fourth Crusade could never be reversed and by the end of the thirteenth century led to their defeat and expulsion from the Holy Land.

An Organizational

Chapter 4 Nightmare

T HE DIFFICULTIES INVOLVED in organizing a military expedition to a faraway land weighed heavily against any chance of success for the crusading movement. Even from the start the Crusades were doomed to failure purely from the standpoint of logistics—the art of moving troops and supplying them with whatever they need to wage war. Maps were inaccurate, and navigational instruments were quite crude. Crusades could take up to six years, and crusading armies had to travel long distances—often in excess of fifteen hundred miles—to reach the Holy Land. Early crusaders traveled overland, departing from various points in Europe including France, Italy, and Germany. Coordinating the movements of these vast armies as they traveled separately across Europe and Asia Minor was an organizational nightmare.

The crusaders had to march through extremes of heat and cold, carrying with them all their weapons, armor, and food supplies. They were constantly in danger of being attacked, either by highwaymen in Europe or by the Turks once they reached Asia Minor. Like most armies throughout history, they relied heavily on the local food supply to sustain them as they traveled, but they could not always count on being able to forage enough food from the land. For example, few crops were grown in Palestine, so crusading armies could not gather food as they marched through or camped in the area. Getting enough food presented enormous difficulties, as historian Elizabeth Hallam explains: "The primitive logistics which supported the crusading armies often broke down and the crusaders were reduced to scavenging or looting to supply their most basic needs, or to starvation."[30]

Finally, financing the crusades required a great deal of money. The armor, helmets, horses, and weapons such as swords and lances that each knight needed were expensive, and thousands of knights had to be equipped. Gathering the necessary supplies and transporting them was very costly, especially when crusaders began transporting supplies and people by sea. Raising the money to finance these ventures took an enormous effort and often fell short. Considering the difficulties in organizing, transporting, and paying for the armies and all their provisions, it is surprising that the armies of the First Crusade managed to conquer the Holy Land and set up the four crusader states. But in the end, the logistics of carrying out such a massive venture proved too great an obstacle for the Crusades to succeed.

Difficulty of Overland Travel

During the first two crusades, most of the armies traveled largely overland. The leaders and knights on a crusade commonly traveled on horseback while the vast majority of foot soldiers and peasants traveled on foot. Sometimes people traveled in rough wagons or on mules and oxen, but more often the wagons and animals were used to cart supplies and chests filled with money to pay for necessities along the way. Those unfortunate knights who lost their horses to

Travel was difficult for the crusading armies. Marching soldiers needed to carry their supplies and armor, and peasants usually traveled on foot.

The Crusaders' Journey through Slavonia

Raymond of Toulouse, a count from France, led one of the four major armies of the First Crusade. His army traveled by land from France and across Europe to Constantinople, but met with difficulties even before they got out of Europe. At that time Europe was a lawless place, and travelers risked being robbed by highwaymen even in their own countries. Raymond d'Aguiliers, who traveled with Raymond of Toulouse, wrote that in Slavonia, part of modern-day Croatia in southeastern Europe, the crusaders found the land barren, the inhabitants unfriendly, and the bandits persistent. The following excerpt from the account of Raymond d'Aguiliers is available from the Internet Medieval Sourcebook at www.fordham.edu/halsall/sbook.html:

> While advancing into the land of Slavonia they suffered many losses on the way, especially because it was then winter. For Slavonia was such a desert and so pathless and mountainous that we saw in it neither wild animals, nor birds for three weeks. The inhabitants of the region were so boorish and rude that they were unwilling to trade with us, or to furnish us guidance, but instead fled from their villages and their castles. . . . Nor was it easy amidst steep mountains and thick woods for our armed knights to pursue the unarmed brigands [bandits] who were acquainted with the country. But they suffered them constantly, unable either to fight or to keep from fighting.

harsh weather or difficult terrain en route to the Holy Land had to continue on foot and rely on pack animals as their mounts in battle.

Where the roads were good, an army might manage to cover twenty-five miles a day. But sometimes the roads were either nonexistent or inadequate, as an army of the First Crusade under Duke Godfrey discovered when they set out from Constantinople to Nicaea in 1097. *The Gesta Francorum*, or *Deeds of the Franks*, written by an anonymous participant in the First Crusade, explains how the duke dealt with the situation:

> When the Duke saw that there existed no road by which he could lead his troops as far as Nicaea, for the path that [an earlier army of] the first Crusaders had originally followed was insufficient for such a number of people, he sent on as an advance guard three thousand men, armed with hatchets and swords, whom he ordered to clear and widen this path to make it usable

for our pilgrims as far as Nicaea. They opened a road through the passes of an immense mountain and as they went along they constructed crosses of iron and wood. . . to guide our pilgrims.[31]

Crusading armies had to travel across areas such as the Anatolian Plateau in Asia Minor, which has a harsh climate—snowbound in winter and broiling in summer. In the autumn of 1096, an army of the First Crusade marched from Constantinople to Antioch, which they planned to take from the Turks. The crusaders had to cross the Anti-Taurus Mountains, which rise ten thousand feet above the Anatolian Plateau and contain many difficult and dangerous passes. Crusades historian Steven Runciman explains the difficulties that the crusaders faced as they traveled through these mountains:

> It was now early October, and the autumn rains had begun. The road over the Anti-Taurus was in appalling disrepair; and for miles there was only a muddy path leading up steep inclines and skirting precipices. Horse after horse slipped and fell over the edge; whole lines of baggage animals, roped together, dragged each other down into the abyss. No one dared to ride.

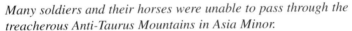

Many soldiers and their horses were unable to pass through the treacherous Anti-Taurus Mountains in Asia Minor.

The knights, struggling on foot under their heavy [armor], eagerly tried to sell their arms to more lightly equipped men, or threw them away in despair. The mountains seemed accursed.[32]

Many crusaders perished during the difficult journey across Europe and Asia Minor. Peter the Hermit's army lost one-fourth of its members even before it reached Constantinople, and an army of the First Crusade that marched through the Anti-Taurus Mountains in 1100 lost three-fourths of its members. Many crusaders ran out of supplies once they reached Asia Minor, and as they straggled along they became more vulnerable to Turkish archers. Women and children who survived Turkish ambushes were captured and sold into slavery in the East. Many crusaders, discouraged by the danger and hardships they faced on their long journey, lost faith and went home.

Food and Shelter for the Crusaders

The basic necessities of life—food to eat, a place to sleep, and protection from harsh weather—were often impossible for crusaders to find. The crusaders set up camps along the way to the Holy Land, although not everyone had tents or blankets for shelter. The nobles' tents were set up in the center of the camp to protect them against attack. Camping outdoors in unfamiliar terrain was a rugged experience for most crusaders, as this letter home from a participant in the First Crusade suggests: "We have endured many sufferings and innumerable evils. Many have already spent all they have, and many would have died from starvation if the kindness of God had not saved them. We suffer from excessive cold and enormous amounts of rain."[33]

The armies that traveled overland had to gather most of their food along the way, and during the First Crusade they resorted to pillaging towns near their route. To gather enough food to meet their needs, the crusaders had to keep on the move because few medieval villages in Europe had enough surplus food supplies to feed a large army. By the Second Crusade, the leaders began arranging to buy food supplies from rulers of lands they would travel through, so pillaging became less of a problem.

Because the crusaders could not always count on there being a supply of safe drinking water in the lands they passed through, they took wine along with them. The crusaders faced a hard choice—drunkenness or disease. Excess consumption of wine commonly led to drunkenness, which was a problem in times of battle. Dysentery—a disease characterized by diarrhea so severe it can lead to dehydration and death—was caused by bad water and improperly cooked food and was also a common problem.

Sometimes the crusaders were so desperate for water that it cost them in battle. In August 1101 a crusader expedition advanced through Asia Minor without an adequate supply of water. When the

"The Anguish of Thirst"

Although Albert of Aachen never went to the Holy Land, he wrote a detailed account of the First Crusade based on the reports of returning pilgrims. In the following extract from his *Historia Hierosolymitana*, reprinted in Elizabeth Hallam's *Chronicles of the Crusades,* he describes the great suffering of the crusaders as they marched across Asia Minor with inadequate supplies of drinking water:

Then the day came . . . when the great shortage of water became acute among the people. And therefore, overwhelmed by the anguish of thirst, as many as around five hundred people of both sexes gave up the ghost [died] on the same day—so they say who were there. Moreover, horses, donkeys, camels, mules, oxen and many animals suffered the same very painful death from thirst.

Very many pregnant women, their throats dried up, their wombs withered, and all the veins of the body drained by the indescribable heat of the sun and that parched region, gave birth and abandoned their own young in the middle of the highway in the view of everyone.

Many men, falling with the exertion and the heat, gaping with open mouths and throats, were trying to catch the thinnest mist to cure their thirst: it could not help them at all. Even the hawks, no less, tame birds and favourites of high-born princes, were dying of that heat and thirst in the hands of their owners who were carrying them. Dogs as well, who were praiseworthy in the hunter's art, panting with the same torment of thirst, were destroyed by the hands of their masters.

Now, while everyone was thus suffering with this affliction, the river they had longed for and searched for was discovered. As they hurried towards it, each was keen because of his excessive longing to get before the rest in the great press. They set no limit to their drinking and went on until very many who had been weakened—as many men as beasts of burden—died from drinking too much.

The Crusader Sword That Broke

Just before embarking on the Third Crusade in 1189, Richard I was besieged by an angry mob in Italy. He had confiscated a hawk from a peasant on the grounds that hawks were for nobles, not peasants, and then hit the man with the flat of his sword. The blow broke the sword in two. This incident demonstrates the problem with European swords of the time: they were brittle. Bladesmiths had stopped making swords that were strong, sharp, and flexible because a flexible sword was useless against the armor that knights wore in Richard's day. According to Terry Jones and Alan Ereira in their book *Crusades,*

> What was needed now was not a sharp, flexible, slicing blade, but a rigid, pointed, metal bar that would pierce. If the sword flexed, it would not penetrate armour. The down side, as Richard was reminded, was that modern swords were not meant for fencing or for swiping. If you did that, they broke.

> The old arts of the bladesmith had survived in the East, where armour was used much less. Metal twisted and retwisted was used to create swords which had a beautiful watery surface, showing the ripples of up to a million layers of wafer-thin metal. Brought by merchants for distribution through Damascus, this became known as "Damascus steel;" not only was it super-sharp, but the structure of the metal meant that as particles came off the edge (through hitting something, for example), a new edge formed. The Islamic sword was self-sharpening.

expedition got near the city of Heraclea in present-day Turkey, the crusaders were suffering from severe thirst, and "when they glimpsed a glistening body of water, they hurled themselves toward it in complete disarray. Kilij Arslan [the Turkish sultan] was waiting for them on the banks."[34] In their dehydrated state, the crusaders were unable to fight back and were massacred by the Turks.

Transporting Supplies

The crusading armies needed to take a multitude of supplies with them. These supplies included food, tents, blankets, weapons, armor, fodder and horseshoes for horses, cooking equipment, and large chests of money to purchase necessities along the way. Most of their supplies were packed in wagons or carried on the backs of horses, donkeys, mules, and oxen. If their horses and pack animals perished, the crusaders had to carry their own armor and other supplies in sacks on their shoulders.

A knight needed to bring along his sword, lance, shield, and armor. Weaponry also included arrows, crossbows, daggers, axes, flails, spiked clubs, and mallets. Lances were simple wood poles, ten to twelve feet long, each with a steel point. The infantry used spears about nine feet long. The crusaders' equipment was not only big, but also heavy. The plated armor alone could weigh up to sixty pounds, and the head of a battle hammer could weigh twenty pounds.

The chain-mail armor worn in the earlier crusades could be rolled into a small bundle and carried on the back of a saddle, to be slipped on as the need arose. But through the course of the Crusades, plate armor became more commonly used because it offered better protection. As the weapons of the Turks improved, the crusaders had to increase the thickness, and therefore the weight, of their armor. Knights needed help to put on plate armor, and the job took so long that knights of the later crusades had to wear their armor whenever there was any danger of attack. Because the crusaders never knew when they might be ambushed along the way, the knights and foot soldiers had to wear armor and carry their weapons on their person

---

The transition from lightweight chain mail (left) to heavy plate armor (right) afforded knights greater protection.

almost continuously as they traveled overland. This was both cumbersome and wearying, slowing their progress considerably and adding time to an already lengthy trip.

By far the largest weapons that the crusaders used were siege engines, which used various methods to hurl objects such as stones, burning hay, and even dead horses over castle walls. One type of siege engine, the mangonel, used a long lever arm with a sling attached by ropes to one end to hold the projectile. Early mangonels used a team of men to pull down on the other end of the lever arm to swing the projectile up and out. Later versions, known as counterweight mangonels or trebuchets, used heavy weights on the lever arm that were lifted by various means and then released. This use of gravity produced a much faster and stronger movement of the lever arm and increased the range to as much as three hundred yards.

The crusaders had to either transport beams and ropes from Europe or obtain them in the Holy Land—which was very expensive—and build their siege engines there. Siege engines were also shipped to the Holy Land, and in more than one crusade the ships themselves were broken apart to provide extra wood for siege engines. Once en-

A siege machine, or catapult, is used to throw large boulders over the walls of cities under attack.

A Shipwreck on the First Crusade

Fulcher of Chartres, who traveled with Count Stephen of Blois in an army of the First Crusade, wrote an account of their journey to the Holy Land. In the fall of 1096 the army marched to southern Italy with the intention of sailing across the Adriatic Sea to modern-day Albania and continuing the march overland to Constantinople. However, with winter approaching, the local sailors refused to risk the crossing. So the crusaders traveling with Count Stephen wintered nearby, and in March of 1097 they were ready to sail. Unfortunately, one of the ships sank, and the tragedy left many of the crusaders reluctant to try a sea journey. This account from Fulcher of Chartres, reprinted in Elizabeth Hallam's Chronicles of the *Crusades: Eye-Witness Accounts of the Wars between Christianity and Islam*, describes the shipwreck and its aftermath:

> When spring returned the duke of Normandy and Count Stephen of Blois took to sea once more with all their followers. When a fleet was finally ready, on 5 April, which happened to be Easter Day, they boarded ship at the harbour of Brindisi on the eastern coast of Italy. Oh how deep and inscrutable are the decisions of God: for before our very eyes, one of the ships suddenly split in the middle, still close to the shore, for no apparent reason.
>
> Four hundred men and women drowned. . . .
>
> Of the remainder who struggled with death, very few survived. The horses and the mules were drowned and a great deal of money was lost.
>
> We were confused and terrified by the sight of this misfortune, to the extent that many who were weak in heart and had not yet boarded ship returned home, giving up the journey, saying they would never trust themselves again to the deceptive and treacherous sea.

gaged in warfare, the crusaders had to cart their siege engines to the castle they were besieging or else cart the timber and ropes and construct them on the spot.

Traveling by Ship

Another means of traveling to the Holy Land was to ship crusading armies, horses, and supplies to their destination. Crusade leaders began making contracts for sea transport with shippers in Italian ports as early as the First Crusade. The shippers agreed to supply fodder for the horses and food and wine or water for the armies. Crusade leaders also built up food supplies and had them shipped in advance to the Holy Land or else brought them along. During the Third Crusade, Richard I transported the supplies for his army in his own ships: large quantities of bacon, beans, cheese, flour, biscuits, wine, syrups, and other foodstuffs. In addition, large quantities of military equipment were also shipped, including crossbows and bolts, bows and arrows, armor, horseshoes, stakes, and beams.

Traveling by ship helped solve some of the problems of traveling overland by eliminating the need for crusaders to make long marches across difficult terrain while carrying all their provisions. However, shipping was very expensive and was not without difficulties of its own. For example, an army of the First Crusade set sail from southern Italy in 1097 and was shipwrecked before it even got out of the harbor. The army lost four hundred men and women along with their horses, mules, and many chests of money. By the Third Crusade, armies were relying more and more extensively on shipping as a means of transport, but shipping still could not eliminate all the transportation problems of the crusaders. For instance, Louis IX sailed to Egypt during the Seventh Crusade, but his fleet of sailing ships was not equipped for a beach landing. The ships grounded in the waters off Egypt, and the knights were forced to wade ashore, carrying all their equipment and supplies with them. John of Joinville, a knight who participated in the Seventh Crusade, wrote that after King Louis's ship grounded, the king himself "jumped into the sea. In water up to his armpits, with his shield around his neck, his helmet on his head and holding his sword, he waded towards his people standing on the beach."[35]

Even shipping supplies to the Holy Land did not solve the problems of getting enough food to the crusaders, because supply ships were prone to being captured or sunk by Muslim forces. When the Muslims intercepted the supply ships for the Seventh Crusade in 1250, the crusaders fighting in Cairo suffered from famine and disease. With their supplies cut off, the weakened army was forced to surrender to the Muslims.

After the establishment of the crusader states during and after the First Crusade, an alternative to transporting supplies was to buy them from the Frankish settlers in the Holy Land. But this was not always practical, as historian Simon Lloyd explains: "Crusaders could, of course, hope to buy provisions, arms, horses, and other necessaries in the

Holy Land, but surviving accounts reveal how expensive this could be with the descent of crusading forces pushing prices up sharply."[36]

Financing the Crusades

Going on crusade required an enormous amount of money. Some knights could afford to pay their own way, but many knights and foot soldiers had to rely on gifts and loans from nobles and kings to pay for their armor, weapons, and other supplies. According to Lloyd, "Finance was always a constant source of worry to all crusaders at all social levels. Moreover, crusades were not self-financing ventures; although the quantities of plunder and booty could be spectacular, they rarely outweighed expenditure and losses."[37]

Louis IX, king of France.

King Louis IX spent an enormous amount of money on the Seventh and Eighth Crusades. In the fourteenth century, the French government estimated that the Seventh Crusade cost Louis 1.5 million livres, which was six times his annual budget. However, there were other costs that the government did not take into account, which meant Louis probably spent double that amount, or twelve times his annual budget. Some of these additional expenses included food and clothing for the king's household; pay for crossbowmen, sergeants at arms, knights, and foot soldiers; gifts and loans to knights; shipping; purchase and replacement of war-horses and mules; and ransom for captives—including the king, who was captured by the Muslims in 1250. Lords, knights, and their households also had their individual expenses. The overall costs of King Louis's two crusades were so great that they continued to burden the French economy for many years after the crusading movement died out.

While many of the early knights and foot soldiers had paid their own way, by the time of the Seventh Crusade, soldiers had begun to

serve for pay, adding greatly to the expense of the crusading movement. Shipping contracts with Genoese and Venetian merchants, who
controlled sea trade and travel in the Mediterranean, also added to
the expense. As the Crusades became more and more costly, finding
additional ways to help finance them became necessary.

Crusade Fund-Raising

Throughout the Crusades, private gifts and loans helped finance the
expeditions. European kings and the Church also found various
means to raise money for the Crusades. Chests were placed in all
churches for the faithful to deposit coins, and these funds contributed to the crusading effort. But by far the greatest fund-raising
sources were taxes—imposed both by secular rulers and by the
Church—and a policy of allowing people to redeem their crusade
vows for cash.

During the twelfth century, European kings and the Church instituted taxation as a means of helping finance the Crusades. One tax,

*A cleric (second man from the left) collects taxes from peasants. Taxes
helped fund the Crusades.*

known as the Saladin tithe, was instituted in England and France in 1188. Named after the great Muslim leader Saladin, the tithe required all subjects in both kingdoms to pay one-tenth of their yearly income in tax. The Saladin tithe produced an enormous amount of money that contributed greatly to the Third Crusade, but it and other secular taxes were unpopular and did not last long.

Papal taxation, on the other hand, raised significant amounts of money throughout the crusading movement. In 1199 Pope Innocent III decreed that all clergy must pay one-fortieth of their revenues for one year in support of the Fourth Crusade, and similar taxation was decreed in support of subsequent crusades. The sums that papal taxation raised were huge. For example, the French church raised nearly 1 million livres for the Seventh Crusade.

Another method that the Church used to raise funds was that of vow redemption—allowing people who took the cross to fulfill their vows and receive an indulgence by contributing money rather than actually participating in a crusade. The policy began in 1213, and by the mid-thirteenth century the vast majority of those taking the cross were urged to redeem their vows. Initially instituted as a means of controlling the large number of noncombatants who went on crusade, the policy of redeeming vows for cash became the largest source of revenue for the later crusades.

Scarce Supplies

Even with all the fund-raising activities going on in Europe, money and supplies were often scarce. The undersupplied crusaders often suffered from thirst and hunger, not only during their travels but also during battle. The French epic poem by Richard the Pilgrim, *Chanson d'Antioche*, gives an account of the crusaders' plight during their siege of Antioch in 1098:

> Starved of supplies, the Christian forces were suffering badly. No one could give aid to another in word or deed. At this time the absence of provisions caused such distress that the Christians were forced to eat their pack-horses in desperation. Through hunger, even fine Spanish war-horses were killed and eaten. Knights and sergeants, fair young girls alike, all rent their garments and cried out in a loud voice:

"God who died on the cross for us, come to our aid!"

Many were weak and fainting through hunger.[38]

One reason for the scarcity of supplies was that much of the money raised for the crusaders never reached them. Fraud, theft, and rulers keeping funds for themselves were all common problems in the Middle Ages. In addition, crusade funds were often diverted to other wars going on in Europe at the time—for example, the battles being waged to drive the Muslims out of Spain. The result was that not all the money that was raised actually went toward the crusading effort in the Holy Land.

The scarcity of funds made it difficult to raise sufficient armies and provide adequate supplies for them. Crusade leaders also had problems coming up with enough money to pay for shipping soldiers and supplies to their destination. The problem of inadequate supplies often led to foraging in the countryside, which was dangerous because the Turks often ambushed foraging parties. The crusaders also ransacked towns to obtain food. One chronicler of the First Crusades wrote an account of an army under the leadership of Bohemond who journeyed through Castoria, a Christian city in present-day Greece. When they arrived they were short on supplies. The account states: "We remained there for several days and sought a market, but the people were unwilling to accord it to us, because they feared us greatly, thinking that we came not as pilgrims, but to devastate their land and to kill them. Wherefore we took their cattle, horses, asses, and everything that we found."[39]

In addition to taking food and other necessities, foraging parties also frequently looted treasures from the villages and towns they passed through, even in Christian lands. This looting of food supplies and treasures gave crusaders a bad reputation, and as the Crusades progressed, villagers were increasingly reluctant to offer crusaders food or shelter. This lack of willing assistance added to the difficulties of transporting and supplying the crusader armies. Though it is clear today that the mounting problems of crusaders and their leaders meant that the movement was doomed to failure, efforts to take and keep the Holy Land persisted until the end of the thirteenth century.

The Final Defeat

O NE OF THE primary goals of the Crusades was to take Jerusalem from the Muslims. The crusaders knew it would be impossible to control the city as an isolated outpost, surrounded by Muslim neighbors who saw the city as belonging to them and who would be intent on retaking it. Therefore, to conquer and hold Jerusalem, the crusaders had to conquer and control the surrounding territory in Syria, Lebanon, and Palestine, including such important cities as Edessa, Antioch, and Acre. At first, the crusaders were successful. They captured land around and north of Jerusalem and established the crusader states. Eventually, though, the Muslims attacked the crusader states and began recapturing their territory, thereby weakening the crusaders' defensive system for Jerusalem.

Some cities in the Holy Land changed hands many times throughout the Crusades. For example, the city of Jerusalem was captured by the crusaders in 1099, recaptured by the Muslims in 1187, recovered by the crusaders in 1229, and lost to the Muslims in 1244. Other cities in the Holy Land were held firmly by the crusaders for nearly two hundred years before the Muslims recaptured them. Even after the failure of the Eighth Crusade in 1272, which proved to be the last major crusade, the final crusader outposts survived another twenty years. But after the fall of Acre—the last Christian-held city in the Holy Land—in 1291, the recovery of Jerusalem or any other crusader territory became a hopeless fantasy. Ultimately, the crusaders failed to hold on to Jerusalem because it was impossible for them to maintain and defend the crusader states.

The Templars and Hospitallers

Several military religious orders were founded during the crusading era. These orders consisted of knights whose duties were to perform religious, military, and charitable functions. The earliest of the military orders was the Knights Templar, founded in Jerusalem around 1120. The Templars' duties extended to defending Christian pilgrims in the Holy Land and supplying part of the Christian military forces against Islam. The Hospital of St. John (known as the Hospitallers), founded in the mid–eleventh century, began as a hospital and later joined the Templars in fulfilling a military role.

The Templars and Hospitallers were the only regular army in the crusader states, and they supplied troops that were more experienced and better disciplined than the knights from the West. Their military experience was often put to good use by placing them in the front and rear of a crusading force in battle. About half of the twelve hundred knights who fought in the Battle of Hattin in 1187 were members of these two orders.

In the early twelfth century, leaders in the crusader states lacked sufficient troops of their own to defend their fortresses, and so the Templars and Hospitallers were both entrusted with the responsibility for the defense of a number of castles and other strongholds in the crusader states. However, the two military orders lost most of their castles after the Battle of Hattin in 1187, in which the Muslims under Saladin were victorious.

By the thirteenth century the military orders were subject to widespread criticism, being accused of pride, avarice, mismanagement of their wealth, and using force against fellow Christians. Historian Alan Forey, in *The Oxford History of the Crusades*, writes that the Templars and Hospitallers

> were turning their weapons on each other because of the bitter rivalry which was thought to exist between them. Rivalry was further seen to hamper fruitful co-operation in battle. Effective military action against Muslims in the East was also thought to be hindered by the independence enjoyed by the orders, while another claim was that military orders in the eastern Mediterranean region were reluctant to pursue aggressive policies towards the infidel. . . . They were in fact thought by some to be on rather too friendly terms with the Muslims.

After the fall of Acre in 1291, the military orders were driven out of the Holy Land along with the last of the settlers. The Templars, the Hospitallers, and St. Thomas of Acre all moved their headquarters to the nearby island of Cyprus. Although the three orders had lost their primary purpose—the defense of Palestine—they continued to lead expeditions against Islam from their island garrisons in the following years. However, without a foothold on the mainland and lacking the support of crusading armies from the West, their efforts to recover the Holy Land were unsuccessful.

The Crusader States

The armies of the First Crusade captured a thin strip of territory along the western coast of Palestine and Syria and established four crusader states there. These states, each of which bore the name of its capital city, consisted of the County of Edessa, the Principality of Antioch, the County of

Latin States After the First Crusade

SULTANATE OF RUM

ASIA MINOR

CAESAREA

KONYA

CILICIA

MARASH

Taurus Mountains

TARSUS   ADANA

EDESSA

ANTIOCH   ALEPPO

Euphrates

ASSASINS

CYPRUS
(BYZANTINE)

KRAK DES CHEVALIERS

TRIPOLI

BEIRUT

SYRIA

Mediterranean   Sea

TYRE

DAMASCUS

ACRE

Sea of Galilee

ARSUF

JAFFA

JERUSALEM

DAMIETTA

GAZA

SELJUQ TURKS

DEAD SEA

EGYPT

FATIMIDS

CAIRO   SUEZ

Nile

SINAI   AQABA

	County of Edessa
	Principality of Antioch
	County of Tripoli
	Kingdom of Jerusalem

Tripoli, and the Kingdom of Jerusalem. The first crusader state to be established was the County of Edessa, in March 1098. The army then marched 160 miles southwest to the city of Antioch, which fell in June 1098 after a nine-month siege. Continuing southward, the crusaders captured Jerusalem in July 1099. Tripoli, the capital of the last crusader state to be established, was under siege for more than five years before it was captured in July 1109. In the space of only eleven years, the crusaders had carved out a Christian kingdom in the Holy Land that stretched nearly six hundred miles along the coast of the Mediterranean Sea, from the Taurus Mountains and the Euphrates River in the north to the Red Sea in the south.

Although necessary to the defense of Jerusalem, the crusader states were vulnerable to attack because of their location. They were spread along a narrow strip of land along the Mediterranean coast, and when attacked they had their backs against the sea. The crusaders were therefore vulnerable to being driven into the sea by Muslim forces attacking from land. Moreover, the crusader states were isolated from Europe, which meant that getting reinforcements sent to help defend against an attack was a lengthy process.

Throughout their two-hundred-year presence in Palestine, the Franks had to defend their lands many times against attacking Muslim forces. Their defense was hampered by a decline in population in the crusader states and lack of cooperation among their rulers. These problems contributed directly to the fall of the crusader states.

A Lack of Defenders

One factor in the fall of the crusader states was a lack of settlers to help defend important cities and fortresses. Though the crusaders had built impressive castles to defend captured territory, there were simply not enough soldiers available to garrison them. As William of Tyre, a twelfth-century historian of the Kingdom of Jerusalem, explains, "Walls, towers, and ramparts avail but little if there are none to man them." [40]

Throughout the Crusades, the population of the crusader states was hard to maintain. Although many thousands of people wanted to go on crusade, most chose not to remain in Palestine. Once their vows had been fulfilled, crusaders wanted to return home to their wives and lands back in Europe. Many of the songs that have survived from the crusading era, such as the French song "Ah! Amours" from 1188, show that crusaders missed their loved ones and longed to return to them. In the first lines of

Frankish Medicine

Medical practices in Islamic countries were far more advanced than those in Europe and the crusader states at the time of the Crusades. Some European practices, such as bleeding and trepanning (drilling a hole in the skull), weakened the patient and often led to infection or death. Not surprisingly, the Franks who settled in the Holy Land brought their largely ineffectual medical practices with them. In his memoir, *An Arab-Syrian Gentleman and Warrior in the Period of the Crusades*, Usamah Ibn-Munqidh recorded the observations of an Arab physician who witnessed some examples of Frankish medicine:

> They brought before me a knight in whose leg an abscess had grown; and a woman afflicted with imbecility. To the knight I applied a small poultice until the abscess opened and became well; and the woman I put on [a] diet. . . . Then a Frankish physician came to them and said, "This man knows nothing about treating them." He then said to the knight, "Which wouldst thou prefer, living with one leg or dying with two?" The latter replied, "Living with one leg." The physician said, "Bring me a strong knight and a sharp ax." A knight came with the ax. And I was standing by. Then the physician laid the leg of the patient on a block of wood and bade the knight strike his leg with the ax and chop it off at one blow. Accordingly he struck it—while I was looking on—one blow, but the leg was not severed. He dealt another blow, upon which the marrow of the leg flowed out and the patient died on the spot. He then examined the woman and said, "This is a woman in whose head there is a devil which has possessed her. Shave off her hair." Accordingly they shaved it off and the woman began once more to eat their ordinary diet—garlic and mustard. Her imbecility took a turn for the worse. The physician then said, "The devil has penetrated through her head." He therefore took a razor, made a deep cruciform [cross-shaped] incision on it, peeled off the skin at the middle of the incision until the bone of the skull was exposed and rubbed it with salt. The woman also expired instantly.

the song, a departing crusader grieves over his imminent departure when he says:

Ahi! Amours, con dure departie
me convendra faire pour le meillour
ki onques fust amee ne servie!
Deus me ramaint a li par sa douçour
si voirement que m'en part a dolour.[41]

With these words, the crusader tells the woman he loves that leaving is enormously difficult and painful for him. He asks that God return him safely to his love when his duty is done. As the song continues, it warns that those who are able but refuse to join the journey for God will suffer dishonor. And then the words of the song return to their earlier romantic tone by saying that no matter what happens to the crusader, or where he ends up, his loved ones will be foremost in his thoughts.

Another problem in maintaining the population of the crusader states was a lack of economic incentive for people to remain there. Despite the lure of the "promised land" that had brought so many people there, expecting a life of wealth and luxury, most people who settled in the Holy Land were disappointed by the realities they found. Much of the land in the crusader states was infertile and unculti-

Knights invade a fortress by building towers that allow them to walk over the top of the wall.

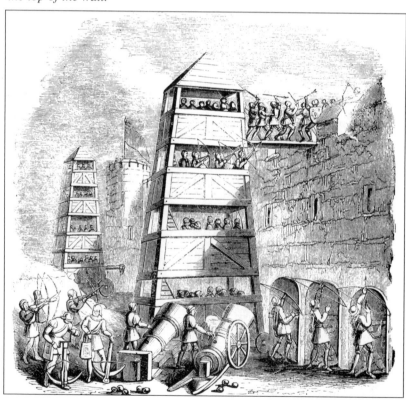

vated—grain had to be imported—and although there were plenty of sheep, goats, pigs, and olive groves, there were not enough products available in the area to provide a good income to the settlers through trade. Most of the items that were produced could be found elsewhere, in larger quantities and at lower prices. For example, Italian merchants bought silks and linens in places other than the crusader states, such as Egypt, and traded them with the rest of Europe.

The crusader states raised money through taxes levied on items that passed through their territory from nearby Muslim countries or the Far East. But in the thirteenth century, Mongol invasions in China, central Asia, Persia, and Syria disrupted trade routes, and the economy of the crusader states began to decline steadily. With the decline in the local economy, the crusader states could not afford to hire enough professional soldiers to defend their frontiers and fortresses, and this, combined with insufficient numbers of settlers, greatly weakened their defenses. Each new crusade brought thousands of new knights and foot soldiers to defend the outposts, but afterward they did not want to settle—and settlers were desperately needed to maintain the strength of the crusader states.

The crusader states in the Holy Land also lost settlers to Constantinople, which after 1204 was under the control of the crusaders. Constantinople was more prosperous and less vulnerable to attack from the Turks than the crusader states were. Some knights who wanted to increase their fortunes through trade actually left Palestine for Constantinople, attracted by its prosperity and relative safety. And many settlers who might otherwise have gone to the Holy Land headed instead to Constantinople. This further drained settlers from the crusader states and left them even more vulnerable to attack.

Calls for new crusades to bring in additional troops to help defend the crusader states fell short because of the decline of popular support and enthusiasm in Europe for the crusading movement. The armies of thirteenth-century crusades were smaller than those of previous crusades. For example, the army Edward I of England commanded in the Holy Land in 1270 consisted of fewer than three hundred knights and only six hundred infantry. Furthermore, the later crusading armies lacked the support of the Byzantine Empire, which had been a bulwark against Muslim advance for centuries. After the crusaders sacked Constantinople in 1204, the Byzantine government

The Second Crusade and the Kingdom of Jerusalem

The Second Crusade was led by Conrad III of Germany and Louis VII of France. Despite careful preparations in France and Germany for the crusade, which included imposing taxes, building roads and bridges, and planning to have the two armies travel at different times so as not to strain the supplies along the way, no one bothered to consult with the Frankish rulers of the crusader states about strategy or goals. This omission had disastrous consequences for the crusade.

The combined forces of Conrad and Louis reached the Kingdom of Jerusalem in 1148, where the two kings argued between themselves and with the local Frankish barons over which city to attack. It was finally decided to attack Damascus. The Frankish barons wanted to add Damascus to their own kingdom and were disappointed to learn that Conrad and Louis planned to give control of the city to another European ruler, the wealthy Count Thierry of Flanders. The attack began in July 1148, and the crusaders quickly had control of the orchards that surrounded Damascus. Then, on the advice of the Frankish barons, the crusaders moved from the orchards to an exposed plain that had no water and faced a well-fortified section of the city wall. The Muslims immediately reoccupied the orchards, and the crusaders were forced into retreat after only five days of fighting.

The humiliating defeat at Damascus was largely due to the mistrust and conflicting interests among the two European leaders, the local barons, and their respective armies. The twelfth-century Crusades historian William of Tyre writes that the local barons had purposely given the crusaders bad advice during the siege because they would rather see the Muslims keep Damascus than see it given to another European count, who would likely turn it into a rival kingdom. After the failure to take Damascus, the Latin Kingdom of Jerusalem was weakened because the crusaders began to mistrust their leaders. In the book *Crusades* by Terry Jones and Alan Ereira, William of Tyre explains that the crusaders

> justly declined all [the leaders'] plans as treacherous and showed utter indifference about the affairs of the kingdom. . . . Their influence caused others who had not been present there to slacken in love towards the kingdom. As a result, fewer people, and those less fervent in spirit, undertook this pilgrimage thereafter. Moreover, even to the present day, those who come fear lest they be caught in the same toils. . . . From this time on, the condition of the Latins in the East became visibly worse.

that relocated to Nicaea was hostile to the crusaders and unwilling to send troops to help the crusader states defend themselves against the Muslims.

A Lack of Cooperation

The four crusader states that were established in the Holy Land were set up according to the European feudal system. Although the Kingdom of Jerusalem claimed sovereignty over the other three states, each retained a degree of independence. Within each state, lands were granted in fiefs to be ruled by barons or knights. Peasants swore their allegiance to the knights, and knights swore their allegiance to the king or prince of each state.

Under the feudal system, peasants work the land granted to them by a baron or knight.

Society in the crusader states mirrored that of Europe, and the problem of knights and kings fighting one another for territory that was so common in Europe also existed in the Holy Land. Continual conflict arose among the Frankish rulers over the boundaries of their states and succession to their thrones. The tensions and warfare within the crusader states often made it difficult for the settlers to co-operate with one another on military matters when they went on the offensive during subsequent crusades and when they were attacked by the Muslims. This lack of cooperation among the Frankish rulers further imperiled the crusader states.

In the early 1140s, for example, the Frankish rulers of the County of Edessa and the Principality of Antioch quarreled over Muslim ter-ritory that each was trying to conquer and add to his own kingdom. The two rulers were not on speaking terms with one another, and this situation put them in a weakened position, vulnerable to outside at-tack. It was at this critical time that the Muslim leader Zangi decided to invade, and he chose the weakest spot in the crusader states to be-gin his attack.

Mameluk Warriors

The Mameluks, whose name means "owned" in Arabic, were Turkish slave-soldiers. By the thirteenth century, the Muslims relied heavily on Mameluk warriors, whose military skill was a decisive factor in the fall of the crusader states. One of the most famous Mameluk warriors was Baybars, who led the force that defeated the crusading army un-der Louis IX at El Mansûra in 1250.

The Mameluks were bought as children and removed from their no-madic life in the central Asian steppes. In Egypt, they were converted to Islam and given intensive military training. Once they were old enough to fight as warriors, they were given their freedom and could rise to any position in the military. In their book *Crusades*, Terry Jones and Alan Ereira explain the Mameluk system:

> They could often hardly speak Arabic. They could marry, but their children could not be Mameluks. Their children were Moslems, and therefore not enslavable, but more importantly, they were unsuitable because they had not been weaned in the wild steppes and then removed from everything they knew. The Mameluk sys-tem needed a constant supply of freshly bought children.

First Blow: The Fall of Edessa

The County of Edessa was the northernmost of the crusader states, which were shaped roughly like a lowercase letter r with Edessa sticking out to the east. Its location made it strategically important to the survival of the other three crusader states because it served as a buffer zone between Christian and Muslim territories. If Edessa fell, the remainder of the crusader states would be left more vulnerable to attack. But Edessa's location also made it the weakest of the crusader states. It was exposed to Turkish lands on all sides except for its border with the Principality of Antioch, and it was under constant threat of Muslim attack.

Zangi began his invasion by capturing several crusader castles in outlying areas of the Principality of Antioch, along its border with the County of Edessa. This put the territory between Antioch and Edessa in Muslim control and further weakened Edessa by driving a wedge between it and the only crusader state with which it shared a border. Edessa was nearly surrounded by the Turks.

In 1144 Zangi decided to attack the city of Edessa, choosing a time when the Frankish ruler, Count Joscelin, was away from the city. Joscelin decided not to return to Edessa, instead occupying nearby Turbessel to prevent Muslim reinforcements from reaching Zangi's army. Joscelin was also counting on the rulers of Jerusalem and Antioch to come to Edessa's aide. Antioch was closer, but because of the animosity between Joscelin and Count Raymond of Antioch, Raymond did not raise an army for Edessa's defense. In fact, Raymond was happy to see Joscelin lose his capital to Zangi. The ruler of Jerusalem did raise an army for Edessa, but by the time it made the long march north, it was too late. Edessa had already fallen, and Zangi ordered all the Franks in the city to be executed. The medieval historian Michael the Syrian describes the ruination of Edessa by Zangi's army:

> Edessa remained a desert: a moving sight covered with a black garment, drunk with blood, infested by the very corpses of its sons and daughters! Vampires and other savage beasts ran and entered the city at night in order to feast on the flesh of the massacred, and it became the abode for jackals; for none entered there except those who dug to discover treasures.[42]

The loss of Edessa was the first major setback to affect the crusader states. In almost fifty years in the Holy Land, the crusaders had never lost any major city to the Muslims. Now Edessa had fallen, and news of its loss stunned people in Europe as well as in the crusader states. Pope Eugenius III responded to the catastrophe by calling for the Second Crusade. But the Second Crusade failed to recapture Edessa, and by 1151 the entire County of Edessa had fallen to the Muslims. The rest of the crusader states were left in a weakened position because there was no longer a buffer zone between them and the Turks.

After Zangi's death in 1146, the Muslim tribes descended into chaos and civil war. But in the mid–thirteenth century a new Muslim leader, Baybars, rose to power and renewed the campaign to drive the Christians out of the Holy Land. Cities and fortresses fell to Baybars in rapid succession, until the Principality of Antioch, the County of Tripoli, and the Kingdom of Jerusalem were reduced to their capitals and a few key cities along the coast. Antioch fell to Baybars in 1268, and Tripoli fell to Baybars's successor, al-Mansur Qalawun, in 1289. After the fall of Tripoli, the only major Christian-held city in the Holy Land was Acre. If Acre fell to the Muslims, it would mean the end of the Christian presence in the Holy Land.

Final Blow: The Fall of Acre

Acre had served as the capital of the kingdom since the city of Jerusalem had fallen to the Muslims a century before. As long as the Franks remained in control of Acre, there could be some hope for the recovery of the holy city of Jerusalem. But without their best port and with no foothold on the mainland, the Crusaders would not be able to succeed in an invasion to recover Jerusalem or any of the other Christian holdings in the Holy Land.

Soon after the fall of Tripoli, the final assault on Acre began. The odds at Acre were overwhelming. The Muslims had 60,000 cavalrymen and 160,000 foot soldiers, and the crusaders had 1,000 knights and 14,000 foot soldiers guarding nearly 40,000 civilians inside the city. As the Muslim forces under al-Ashraf battered their way through the city walls, the last crusader ruler of Acre, King Henry, deserted the city and fled with his nobles and their families to take refuge on the nearby island of Cyprus. A knight called the Templar

Mameluk Siege Warfare: Sapping

The siege warfare of the Mameluks was one of the most decisive factors that brought about the final downfall of the Franks in the crusader states. The Mameluks employed a method of storming crusader fortresses known as "sapping." This process, in which the Mameluks dug a tunnel up to the foundation of the outer castle wall, is described by Usamah Ibn-Munqidh in his memoir, *An Arab-Syrian Gentleman and Warrior in the Period of the Crusades.*

> On the sides of the tunnel were set up two pillars, across which stretched a plank to prevent the earth above it from falling down. The whole tunnel had such a framework of wood that extended as far as the foundation of the barbican [castle wall]. Then the assailants dug under the wall of the barbican, supported it in its place, and went as far as the foundation of the tower. The tunnel was narrow. As soon as they got to the tower, they enlarged the tunnel in the wall of the tower, supported it on timbers and began to carry out, a little at a time, the splinters of stone produced by boring. . . .

> They then began to cut dry wood and stuff the tunnel with it. Early the next morning they set it on fire. We had just at that time put on our arms and marched, under a great shower of stones and arrows, to the trench in order to make an onslaught on the castle as soon as its tower tumbled over. As soon as the fire began to have its effect, the layers of mortar between the stones of the wall began to fall. Then a crack was made. The crack became wider and wider and the tower fell.

The use of sapping increased greatly in the last half of the thirteenth century as the Mameluks set about obliterating the Frankish strongholds. The Mameluks' aim was not to salvage the castles to refortify them for their own use, as was sometimes done by the Muslims, but rather to raze all the crusader fortresses to prevent the Franks from reestablishing themselves in Palestine. Therefore, the Mameluks had become much more aggressive in their sapping efforts, and Frankish fortresses all along the coast fell in a matter of weeks.

---

of Tyre wrote the following eyewitness account of the conquest of Acre, in which the Muslims laid waste to the city and massacred the inhabitants:

> That day was appalling, for nobles and citizens, women and girls were frantic with terror; they went running through the streets, their children in their arms, weeping

A painting depicts the fall of Acre, in which the Muslims reclaimed their city.

and desperate; they fled to the sea-shore to escape death, and when the Saracens caught them one would take the mother and the other the child, they would drag them from place to place and pull them apart; and sometimes two Saracens would quarrel over a woman and she would be killed; or a woman was taken and her suckling child flung to the ground where it died under the horses' hooves.[43]

Those inhabitants of Acre who were not slaughtered were sold into slavery. King Henry and the others who found refuge on the island of Cyprus met with hardship. Steven Runciman writes, "For a generation they lived the miserable lives of unwanted refugees, for whom as the years passed sympathy wore thin."[44] Acre had fallen, and with it the last remnants of the crusader states and the last chance of success for the crusades.

Failure to Recover the Holy Land

Although the fall of Acre represented the final defeat of the crusades, hopes for recovery of Christian territory in the Holy Land remained. Some crusades were attempted after 1291, but they faced overwhelming difficulties. With the crusader states defeated, and without a single Christian fortress in the Holy Land, the possibility of success in recovering Jerusalem or any part of the Holy Land was extremely unlikely. Moreover, after the fall of Acre, the Muslim sultan al-Ashraf destroyed all of the crusader towns and castles to prevent them from being used for any future Christian reconquests. The sultan left nothing but desolation along the coast, destroying orchards, farmsteads, and irrigation systems.

Even after the fall of Acre in 1291 and the systematic destruction of all the crusaders' castles and fortresses, some European rulers continued to hope for recovery of Christian territory in the Holy Land. But by the late thirteenth century, when Acre fell, the crusading spirit that had driven the masses to take the cross in 1095 had died. People in Europe were no longer interested, and most probably shared the opinion of Salimbene of Adam, who wrote in 1274, "It does not seem to be the divine will that the [Church of the] Holy Sepulchre should be recovered, since the great number attempting it are seen to have laboured in vain."[45] After the fall of Acre, attempts to raise armies either failed entirely or resulted in forces that were so small as to have no chance of success.

The crusaders had come very close to achieving their goal of retaking and holding Christian territory in the Holy Land. To the later crusaders, the triumphs of the First Crusade seemed nothing short of miraculous. To march across Asia Minor, ill-equipped and poorly supplied, battle such a formidable foe, capture cities one by one, and set up Christian kingdoms in the midst of Muslim lands seemed to the thirteenth-century crusaders like the work of superhumans. Although the crusaders managed to keep at least a toehold in Palestine for nearly two hundred years, the crusading movement resulted in the

This fortress was built by crusaders in Syria in 1100 and still stands today as a reminder of the Crusades.

deaths of hundreds of thousands of Christians, Muslims, and Jews, disrupted societies in Europe and the Middle East, nearly bankrupted France and other nations, and left a legacy of mistrust between Christians and Muslims that has spawned countless problems for hundreds of years.

The Results of the Crusades

THE STORY OF THE Crusades is a shameful one, marked by brutality, intolerance, and greed. The First Crusaders quickly lost their original idealism as they began to struggle among themselves for power in the conquered lands. The goal of driving the Muslims out of the Holy Land was never reached, and in fact the crusaders so weakened the Christian East by the sack of Constantinople in 1204 that they gave the Turks an open door to the Byzantine Empire. Within 150 years of driving the last of the Franks out of the crusader states, the Turks had conquered Constantinople and were threatening western and central Europe. As historian Franklin Hamilton writes, "When Pope Urban issued his call in 1095, the Seljuk Turks had an uneasy grasp on parts of Asia Minor and Syria. . . . Three and a half centuries later, the Ottoman Turks ruled all the East and much of Europe. There was no gain for Christianity, only a colossal loss."[46]

Although the Crusades ultimately failed to achieve their purpose of retaking and occupying the Holy Land, the centuries of contact between the East and the West led to many cultural, political, and economic changes in Europe. The most sweeping result of the Crusades was an increase in the power and influence of the West. Even though the Muslim world had been victorious in the Crusades, within two centuries European Christians increasingly dominated world political and cultural affairs, exploring and colonizing the New World, while the domination and prestige of the Muslim world faded. The American

A knight returns from a crusade, weary from battle.

scholar M. G. S. Hodgson explains this unexpected result of the Crusades: "Not Muslims but the despised Christians of the far north-west,
long since written off as too cold and fog-bound to produce anything
more intelligent than the unpolished Crusaders that had already come
from there, now suddenly had the mastery in the world's affairs."[47]
The rise of Europe to worldwide power and influence was due in large
part to the increased contact with the Muslim world.

Increased Contact

Some of the seeds of Europe's eventual world dominance came from the Muslim East. The Crusades produced increased contact and trade between East and West, as well as a revival of learning in Europe, and in many ways set the stage for the Renaissance. The crusaders brought back many things from the East, such as new foods, new spices, and even new words—*alchemy, alcohol, algebra, amalgam, cipher*, and *zenith* all have Arabic origins. Through their contact with the Muslim world, the Europeans learned about many things, such as Islamic medicine, astronomy, chemistry, geography, mathematics, and architecture. These fields were all more advanced in the Muslim world, and the Europeans benefited greatly from what they learned. They also learned the process for papermaking, leather working, textiles, distilling alcohol, and refining sugar from the Arabs. The culture of the Greeks, long lost to the Europeans, was also conveyed to them by the Arabs. The Europeans owed much of their later economic success and worldwide cultural influence to the knowledge they gained from the Muslims.

The Crusades played a major role in changing the culture and politics of the world. For the first time, significant numbers of European Christians carried their culture and religion abroad, and the crusader states became the earliest example of the European expansionism and colonialism that would flourish in the centuries to come.

The Renaissance

The Crusades played a major role in the economic revolution that took place in Europe during the Middle Ages. The Italian cities of Venice and Genoa benefited greatly from the crusaders' needs for shipping and supplies. Venice and Genoa both became great commercial centers during the Middle Ages, and the increase in trade items from the East added to their wealth. Products from the East, such as fruits, spices, drugs, dyes, gems, silks, and brocades, reached Europe through the cities of Venice and Genoa, and these items were then traded in other European cities as far north as England. The burgeoning economy of Venice and Genoa helped set the stage for the Renaissance, which had its beginnings in Italy in the fourteenth century and eventually expanded into the rest of Europe.

Venice, Italy, (shown here) was one of the trading cities that gained commercial benefits from the Crusades.

The role of the Crusades in altering Europe during the Middle Ages is undeniable. As Steven Runciman writes, "The era of the Crusades is one of the most important in the history of Western civilization. When it began, western Europe was only just emerging from the long period of barbarian invasions that we call the Dark Ages. When it ended, that great burgeoning that we call the Renaissance had just begun."[48] Although the Crusades were one of history's great defeats, the increase in learning and trade they brought about was a major factor in pulling Europe out of a long period of decline and isolation and in launching the Renaissance, leaving a mark on civilization that cannot be erased.

Notes

Introduction: The Soldiers of Christ

1. Anna Comnena, *The Alexiad of Anna Comnena*. New York: Penguin Books, 1969, p. 309.
2. Quoted in Norman Clare, ed., *Music of the Crusades*, booklet to accompany the compact disc by the Early Music Consort of London. New York: London Records, 1970, p. 9.
3. Quoted in Elizabeth Hallam, ed., *Chronicles of the Crusades: Eye-Witness Accounts of the Wars Between Christianity and Islam*. New York: Welcome Rain, 2000, p. 11.

Chapter 1: The Crusading Movement

4. Malcolm Billings, *The Cross and the Crescent: A History of the Crusades*. New York: Sterling, 1988, p. 19.
5. Quoted in Billings, *The Cross and the Crescent*, p. 18.
6. Quoted in Hallam, *Chronicles of the Crusades*, p. 21.
7. Steven Runciman, *A History of the Crusades*, vol. 3. 1951. Reprint, New York: Cambridge University Press, 1997, p. 480.

Chapter 2: The Doomed Armies of the Crusades

8. Quoted in Hallam, *Chronicles of the Crusades*, p. 82.
9. Amin Maalouf, *The Crusades Through Arab Eyes*. New York: Schocken Books, 1984, p. 5.
10. Comnena, *The Alexiad of Anna Comnena*, p. 312.
11. Anne Fremantle, *Age of Faith*. New York: Time, 1965, p. 60.
12. Hallam, *Chronicles of the Crusades*, p. 242.
13. Quoted in Billings, *The Cross and the Crescent*, p. 141.
14. Quoted in Hallam, *Chronicles of the Crusades*, p. 255.
15. Quoted in Hallam, *Chronicles of the Crusades*, p. 255.
16. Hallam, *Chronicles of the Crusades*, p. 120.

17. Carole Hillenbrand, *The Crusades: Islamic Perspectives.* New York: Routledge, 2000, p. 512.
18. Quoted in Hallam, *Chronicles of the Crusades*, p. 189.

Chapter 3: A Loss of Popular Support

19. Jonathan Riley-Smith, ed., *The Oxford History of the Crusades.* New York: Oxford University Press, 1999, p. 17.
20. Quoted in Hallam, *Chronicles of the Crusades*, p. 68.
21 Maalouf, *The Crusades Through Arab Eyes*, p. xiv.
22. Maalouf, *The Crusades Through Arab Eyes*, p. xiv.
23. Quoted in Francesco Gabrieli, ed., *Arab Historians of the Crusades.* 1957. Reprint, New York: Barnes and Noble, 1993, p. 11.
24. Quoted in Terry Jones and Alan Ereira, *Crusades.* New York: Facts On File, 1995, p. 64.
25. Quoted in Hallam, *Chronicles of the Crusades*, p. 213.
26. Quoted in Hallam, *Chronicles of the Crusades*, pp. 220–221.
27. John Julius Norwich, *A Short History of Byzantium.* New York: Vintage Books, 1997, p. 304.
28. Quoted in Norwich, *A Short History of Byzantium*, pp. 304–305.
29. Norwich, *A Short History of Byzantium*, p. 306.

Chapter 4: An Organizational Nightmare

30. Hallam, *Chronicles of the Crusades*, p. 135.
31. Quoted in Regine Pernoud, ed., *The Crusades.* New York: G. P. Putnam's Sons, 1963, p. 53.
32. Runciman, *A History of the Crusades*, vol. 1, p. 192.
33. Quoted in Jones and Ereira, *Crusades*, p. 57.
34. Maalouf, *The Crusades Through Arab Eyes*, p. 65.
35. Quoted in Hallam, *Chronicles of the Crusades*, p. 268.
36. Quoted in Riley-Smith, *The Oxford History of the Crusades*, p. 63.
37. Quoted in Riley-Smith, *The Oxford History of the Crusades*, p. 54.
38. Quoted in Hallam, *Chronicles of the Crusades*, p. 76.
39. Quoted in Paul Halsall, "The Crusaders' Journey to Constantinople: Collected Accounts," 1997. Available at the Internet Medieval Sourcebook, www.fordham.edu/halsall/sbook.html.

Chapter 5: The Final Defeat

40. Quoted in Jones and Ereira, *Crusades*, p. 102.
41. Quoted in Clare, *Music of the Crusades*, pp. 20–22.

42. Quoted in Riley-Smith, *The Oxford History of the Crusades*, p. 227.

43. Quoted in Hallam, *Chronicles of the Crusades*, pp. 280–81.

44. Runciman, *A History of the Crusades*, vol. 3, p. 423.

45. Quoted in Jonathan Riley-Smith, ed., *The Crusades: A Short History*. New Haven: Yale University Press, 1987, p. 177.

Epilogue: The Results of the Crusades

46. Franklin Hamilton, *The Crusades*. New York: Dial Press, 1965, p. 299.

47. Quoted in Hillenbrand, *The Crusades: Islamic Perspectives*, pp. 611-12.

48. Runciman, *A History of the Crusades*, vol. 3, p. 470.

Chronology

1054
The Great Schism officially divides the Eastern (Orthodox) and the Western (Roman) Churches.

1071
Seljuq Turks capture the city of Jerusalem.

1095
Pope Urban II calls for a crusade to the Holy Land at Council of Clermont.

1096–1102
The First Crusade.

1098
Crusaders capture Edessa and Antioch.

1099
Crusaders capture Jerusalem.

1109
Crusaders capture Tripoli.

1124
Crusaders capture Tyre.

1144
Edessa falls to the Muslims.

1145
Pope Eugenius III proclaims the Second Crusade.

1147–1149
The Second Crusade.

1174
Damascus falls to Saladin.

1183
Aleppo falls to Saladin.

1186
Mosul falls to Saladin.

1187
Crusaders defeated by Muslims at Hattin; Acre and Jerusalem fall to Saladin; Pope Gregory VIII proclaims the Third Crusade.

1189–1192
The Third Crusade.

1191
Crusaders capture Cyprus and Acre.

1198
Pope Innocent III proclaims the Fourth Crusade.

1202–1204
The Fourth Crusade.

1202
Crusaders sack Zara.

1204
Crusaders sack Constantinople.

1213
Pope Innocent III proclaims the Fifth Crusade.

1217–1221
The Fifth Crusade.

1218–1219
Siege of Damietta.

1227–1229
The Sixth Crusade.

1244
Jerusalem falls to the Khorezmians.

1245
Pope Innocent IV calls for the Seventh Crusade.

1248–1254
The Seventh Crusade.

1268
Antioch falls to the Mameluks.

1269–1272

The Eighth Crusade.

1270

King Louis IX of France dies in Tunisia.

1289

Tripoli falls to the Mameluks.

1291

Acre falls to the Mameluks; all crusader castles and cities in Palestine razed.

Glossary

Byzantine Empire: Empire of southeast and southern Europe and western Asia from the fourth to fifteenth centuries, with its capital at Constantinople. Also called the Eastern Roman Empire.

chivalry: The qualities of the ideal medieval European knight, such as courage, courtesy, and consideration—especially toward women—and generosity toward enemies.

Constantinople: The capital of the Byzantine Empire, it was captured and sacked by crusaders in 1204 during the Fourth Crusade, retaken by Byzantines in 1261 under Emperor Michael VIII Palaeologus, and captured in 1453 by Ottoman Turks under Sultan Mehmed II.

crusader states: The four kingdoms set up by the crusaders in lands they conquered in Palestine during the First Crusade; they consisted of the County of Edessa, the Principality of Antioch, the County of Tripoli, and the Kingdom of Jerusalem. These kingdoms fell one by one to Muslim forces beginning in the mid–twelfth century.

Crusades: The series of military expeditions undertaken by Christian powers under papal authority in the eleventh, twelfth, and thirteenth centuries to win the Holy Land from the Muslims.

feudalism: The political, social, and economic system prevalent in Europe from the ninth century to about the fifteenth century in which the lord of a manor offered protection to vassals, or tenants, who in turn pledged loyalty and military service to the lord.

fief: The fee granted by a lord to his vassal, usually in the form of land.

Franks: A term meaning "French" and used by Muslims for all Christian crusaders, irrespective of their nationality.

Greek fire: A composition that exploded into flames on contact.

Greeks: A term used by crusaders from western Europe for inhabitants of the Byzantine Empire.

Holy Land: The area in Asia Minor also known as Palestine. It contains Jerusalem, which is a sacred city to Jews, Christians, and Muslims alike.

indulgence: Complete remission from punishment for sin granted by the pope to those who took the cross (vowed to go on a crusade). Indulgences were a powerful motivator for people to join the Crusades.

infidel: An unbeliever. Christians and Muslims alike used this term for each other.

Islam: The religion founded by the prophet Muhammad in Mecca circa 610.

Jerusalem: The city in Palestine that is most sacred for Jews, Christians, and Muslims. Its recovery was the goal of several crusades. The city changed hands many times after it was captured by the armies of the First Crusade in 1099; it was lost along with nearly all of Palestine to Saladin in 1187, recovered by crusaders at the end of the Fifth Crusade in 1229, and captured by Khorezmian Muslims in 1244.

knight: A mounted and heavily armed soldier serving a feudal superior. Knights were above the peasantry but below the nobles whom they served.

Latins: A term used by the Byzantines for Europeans.

Mameluk: Freed Turkish slaves who were used as soldiers by the Muslims. The Mameluks, led by Baybars, rose to power in Egypt and eventually drove the crusaders out of Palestine.

military orders: Religious orders founded in the early twelfth century whose purpose was to provide defense and care for pilgrims traveling through the Holy Land. The Templars and the Hospitallers, two of the military orders, both provided armies to help fight the Crusades.

mosque: An Islamic building used for public worship and as a community meeting place.

Muslim: A follower of Islam.

penance: An act performed to atone for one's sins.

pilgrimage: A journey to a shrine or a sacred place. During the Middle Ages, pilgrimages to the Holy Land were undertaken as an act of penance.

pope: The head of the Western (Roman) Church.

relic: An object associated with a saint or holy person and held as sacred.

Saracens: A name used by the Byzantines, and subsequently all crusaders, for Muslims.

Seljuq Turks: Formerly nomadic Muslim tribe from the central Asian steppes. By the late eleventh century, the Seljuqs had conquered most of the Byzantine provinces in Asia Minor and captured the city of Jerusalem.

siege engines: Various types of catapults that were used to hurl objects over castle walls.

sultan: A Muslim term for the sovereign leader of a territory or empire.

vassal: A feudal tenant who has vowed loyalty and service to a lord in return for the lord's protection and an estate of land or money.

For Further Reading

Karen Armstrong, *Holy War: The Crusades and Their Impact on Today's World*. New York: Doubleday, 1991. Written by an authority on religious affairs, this book examines how the Crusades continue to influence the way Muslims and Christians view each other in modern times.

———, *Islam: A Short History*. New York: Modern Library, 2000. This book traces the founding, development, and spread of Islam from the seventh century to the present day.

Malcolm Barber, *The Trial of the Templars*. 1978. Reprint, New York: Cambridge University Press, 1998. This book covers the arrest, torture, trial, and execution of the knights of the Order of the Temple during the Inquisition.

Timothy L. Biel, *The Crusades*. San Diego: Lucent Books, 1995. This book covers the history of the Crusades to the Holy Land.

Robert Chazan, *In the Year 1096: The First Crusade and the Jews*. Philadelphia: Jewish Publication Society, 1996. This book chronicles the pogroms against Jews in the Rhineland at the start of the First Crusade.

Penny J. Cole, *The Preaching of the Crusades to the Holy Land, 1095–1270*. Cambridge, MA: Medieval Academy of America, 1991. This book covers the efforts to preach the idea of a holy war against Islam and to recruit people to take the cross.

Evan S. Connell, *Deus Lo Volt!: Chronicle of the Crusades*. Washington, DC: Counterpoint, 2000. This novel gives a historically accurate portrait of the Crusades from the point of view of a European participant.

Christoph T. Maier, *Preaching the Crusades: Mendicant Friars and the Cross in the Thirteenth Century*. New York: Cambridge University Press, 1994. Part of a Cambridge series studying medieval life and thought, this book examines efforts to recruit participants for the later crusades.

Peter Partner, *God of Battles: Holy Wars of Christianity and Islam*. Princeton: Princeton University Press, 1998. This book looks at the religious aspects of the Crusades from both sides, examining the Christian doctrine of holy war and the Islamic doctrine of jihad.

Piers Paul Read, *The Templars*. New York: St. Martin's Press, 1999. This book covers the history of the Templars from the founding of the order in 1119 to the execution of the last two knights in 1314.

Geoffrey Regan, *Lionhearts: Saladin, Richard I, and the Era of the Third Crusade*. New York: Walker, 1999. This book takes an in-depth look at the opposing forces of the Third Crusade: Sultan Saladin of Egypt and Syria, and King Richard I of England.

Earle Rice, *Life During the Crusades*. San Diego: Lucent Books, 1998. This book examines why the Crusades were fought and describes daily life for the Christian West and Muslim East during the Crusades.

Jean Richard, *The Crusades, c. 1071–c. 1291*. New York: Cambridge University Press, 1999. This book covers the history of the First through the Eighth Crusades and chronicles the fall of the crusader states in the East.

Desmond Seward, *The Monks of War: The Military Religious Orders*. New York: Penguin Books, 1995. This is a history of the military religious orders that emerged during the crusading era to wage battle against the forces of Islam.

Bradley Steffens, *The Children's Crusade*. San Diego: Lucent Books, 1991. This book examines the disastrous Children's Crusade of 1212.

Works Consulted

Books

Karen Armstrong, *Muhammad: A Biography of the Prophet*. San Francisco: HarperSanFrancisco, 1992. This biography of the prophet Muhammad, written by an authority on world religions, covers the life and legacy of the founder of Islam.

Malcolm Billings, *The Cross and the Crescent: A History of the Crusades*. New York: Sterling, 1988. This book, which was written to accompany the BBC radio series of the same name, provides views of the Crusades from both Christian and Muslim perspectives.

Norman Clare, ed., *Music of the Crusades*, booklet to accompany the compact disc by the Early Music Consort of London. New York: London Records, 1970. This compact disc contains recordings of nineteen songs in French, German, and Latin that have survived from the crusading era, with the translated lyrics included in the accompanying booklet.

Anna Comnena, *The Alexiad of Anna Comnena*. New York: Penguin Books, 1969. Written by the daughter of Emperor Alexius I Comnenus, this remarkable memoir gives details about the events and people of the early crusading era.

Anne Fremantle, *Age of Faith*. New York: Time, 1965. Part of Time-Life's Great Ages of Man series, this book examines the history of the Middle Ages and includes a chapter on the Crusades.

Francesco Gabrieli, ed., *Arab Historians of the Crusades*. 1957. Reprint, New York: Barnes and Noble, 1993. The author presents a view of the Crusades using accounts from Arab chroniclers and historians of the time.

Frances Gies and Joseph Gies, *Life in a Medieval Village*. New York: Harper and Row, 1990. This book profiles various aspects of life in several medieval English villages.

Elizabeth Hallam, ed., *Chronicles of the Crusades: Eye-Witness Accounts of the Wars Between Christianity and Islam*. New York: Welcome Rain, 2000. This book provides firsthand narratives of the crusading era from both European and Arab perspectives.

———, ed., *Four Gothic Kings*. New York: Weidenfeld and Nicolson, 1987. This book uses the records of medieval chroniclers to illustrate the lives of four thirteenth- and fourteenth-century kings, Henry III, Edward I, Edward II, and Edward III.

Franklin Hamilton, *The Crusades*. New York: Dial Press, 1965. This book covers the history of the Crusades from the Council of Clermont in 1095 to the fall of Acre in 1291.

Carole Hillenbrand, *The Crusades: Islamic Perspectives*. New York: Routledge, 2000. This book examines the Islamic concept of jihad and explains how the Muslims drove the crusaders out of the Holy Land.

Philip K. Hitti, trans., *An Arab-Syrian Gentleman and Warrior in the Period of the Crusades: Memoirs of Usamah Ibn-Munqidh*. New York: Princeton University Press, 2000. This memoir provides a firsthand account of the Crusades from a non-European perspective.

Terry Jones and Alan Ereira, *Crusades*. New York: Facts On File, 1995. Published to accompany the Arts and Entertainment Network series of the same name, this book tells the story of the men, women, and children who took part in the Crusades.

Amin Maalouf, *The Crusades Through Arab Eyes*. New York: Schocken Books, 1984. Using the accounts of Arab eyewitnesses and participants in the battle against the invasion from the West, the author shows how the Muslims defeated the crusaders.

William H. McNeill, *Plagues and Peoples,* New York: Quality Paperback Book Club, 1993. This book discusses the impact of disease on civilizations from prehistoric times through the nineteenth century.

John Julius Norwich, *A Short History of Byzantium*. New York: Vintage Books, 1997. This book gives the history of the Byzantine

Empire from its founding in the fourth century to its fall in the fifteenth century and chronicles the role of the Crusades in the empire's decline.

Regine Pernoud, ed., *The Crusades*. New York: G. P. Putnam's Sons, 1963. Using the accounts of eyewitnesses and participants, this book covers the history of the Crusades from Pope Urban's appeal at Clermont in 1095 to the fall of Acre in 1291.

Jonathan Riley-Smith, ed., *The Crusades: A Short History*. New Haven: Yale University Press, 1987. This book details the reasons behind the call for the First Crusade and gives a history of the crusading movement, from initial victories to eventual demise.

———, *The Oxford History of the Crusades*. Oxford: Oxford University Press, 1999. With each chapter written by a different authority, this book examines aspects of the Crusades such as the origins of the movement, life in the crusader states, and the survival of crusading ideology into the twentieth century.

Steven Runciman, *A History of the Crusades*. 3 vols. 1951. Reprint, New York: Cambridge University Press, 1997. This multivolume history, considered a classic, deals with the rise and fall of the crusading movement.

Internet Source

Paul Halsall, "The Crusaders' Journey to Constantinople: Collected Accounts." The Internet Medieval Sourcebook, www.fordham.edu/halsall/sbook.html.

Index

Picture Credits

About the Author

Cherese Cartlidge is a freelance writer and editor. Cherese attended New Mexico State University, where she received a B.A. in psychology. She and her two children, Olivia and Tommy, have lived in Georgia since 1997.